Endorse

Ray Clark knows how to fight. I know, because we served together in combat. Ray was then–and is today–a "Warrior's Warrior." If you know and love a veteran of today's war–or any other–this book is a "must read."

—Lt. Col. Oliver L. North (USMC Ret.)

Having led the Marines of Kilo Company in 1969, I'm glad to see Ray is writing about the men and events that helped shape both of our lives. This book not only paints a graphic picture of deadly contact with the enemy, but also deals with life after combat. I hope his book will help bring healing to many veterans as it is never too late to help those who are still struggling with combat related Post Traumatic Stress Disorder.

—Col. Paul B. Goodwin (USMC Ret.)

Marines have a well earned reputation for being incredibly tough warriors. They are expected to win our nation's battles, and that is what Marines do. Ray Clark provides vivid descriptions of what life was like for our Marines on the ground in Vietnam in 1969. He also describes the problems that followed some of those young warriors home. The most important thing he does in this book is to tell others who have or are experiencing the same post combat effects that help is available and that it works. Ray showed his toughness in battle and in the ensuing struggle. His book has the potential to be an inspiration to many combat veterans suffering from PTSD. For Ray's valiant effort to assist in the healing process of his fellow warriors, I congratulate him.

—Lt. Gen. Thomas Braaten (USMC Ret.)

This book is one of the best written on Viet Nam and the enduring effects of combat. I served with Ray in Kilo 3/3 in 1969. He
has been in some of the bloodiest battles in Viet Nam. I can
attest to that as I was a Corpsman in some of those battles. As
a Clinical Psychologist I have been treating the psychological
ravages of war since the early 80's. His descriptions of PTSD
and the necessity for proper treatment cannot be overstated. It is
never too late to seek treatment. Our Military Hospitals and the
V.A. have the resources and dedicated clinicians to help you and
your family members. Please ask. We will help you.

—John C. Fowler, Ph.D.
Senior Corpsman
3/3 Kilo Co., 1969

To:

Semper Fi,
Ray & Laura Clark
Kilo 3/3/3

THE
NEVER-ENDING
WAR

THE NEVER-ENDING WAR

THE UNSEEN SCARS OF POST-TRAUMATIC STRESS DISORDER

LM CLARK

TATE PUBLISHING
AND ENTERPRISES, LLC

Published by Tate Publishing & Enterprises, LLC
127 E. Trade Center Terrace | Mustang, Oklahoma 73064 USA
1.888.361.9473 | www.tatepublishing.com

Tate Publishing is committed to excellence in the publishing industry. The company reflects the philosophy established by the founders, based on Psalm 68:11,
"The Lord gave the word and great was the company of those who published it."

Book design copyright © 2013 by Tate Publishing, LLC. All rights reserved.
Cover design by Rodrigo Adolfo
Interior design by Ronnel Luspoc

Published in the United States of America
ISBN: 978-1-62510-921-7
1. Biography & Autobiography / Military
2. Psychology / Psychopathology / Post-Traumatic Stress Disorder (Ptsd)
13.05.13

Dedication

To Ronald E. Clark

The one who helped make this book possible by praying his son through the many close calls and near misses in Vietnam 1969. Without his faithfulness and prayers to a loving God, Ray would have never made it back home.

> I sought the Lord and He heard me and delivered me from all of my fears.
>
> Psalm 34:4, KJV

Acknowledgements

After spending many years thinking and dreaming of writing my memoirs of Vietnam, it has finally happened. The honor of telling the world about the unsung heroes of Kilo Company 3/3/3 in 1969 started with first opening up my memories to my wife, Laura. She has not only encouraged me to record my memories, but she actually helped me write it. I had no trouble remembering the narrative of the story, but writing it down properly was something else. The first problem I ran into was my inability to communicate what I was feeling. I considered the fact that my nerves were bad enough (through my PTSD) without my being criticized and scrutinized by other bona fide writers for my poor writing abilities. I didn't think I could take that kind of pressure, so my wife proposed the idea of me telling my story in detail and her conveying it into a book form. It sounded like a good idea. My excuse was that the marines taught me how to fight, not write. What a lame excuse. I had also been told in the beginning that my writing skills were atrocious, so I decided to let Laura do it.

Contents

Foreword

Dictating Begins

Changing a verbal account of a horrific war story into a picture everyone can clearly see comes with a high cost to the artist whether they have been in combat or not. If the information they have to work with is factual and precise, the picture will come to fruition. We both understood there couldn't be any misunderstandings in the story line because it would take away from what I was trying to convey to the reader. Laura has not only proven to be my closest friend, but now she has traveled with me in time as we have relived my tour of duty in the jungles of Vietnam 1969. It has been a heavy burden for her to bear as she has been subjected to the fear, sights, and sounds of men dying in combat while living in the deadly hot, dirty jungles, mountains, and flatlands in Southeast Asia. Through her being told in a vivid account, she has sensed death in the darkness, ambushed the enemy as they approached unaware, and has even been caught in deadly traps while trying to stay alive for a year of close calls and near misses. I'm sure that the laborious task of writing and rewriting this story many times has taken a toll on her nerves. She has mentally walked beside me as I walked point in the most dangerous areas of Vietnam. We found out that the "meat grinder" is no respecter of persons as it has a unique way of infecting and affecting anyone who dares to go there. I now wouldn't be surprised in the least to find out that she has also developed some form of PTSD from second hand consumption of information. One of the benefits of this book is that I've had a chance to share my hidden life with her and hopefully many others. We both feel passionate about the prospects of reaching other victims with help and support by sharing our struggles and achievements of overcoming the debilitating effects of PTSD. Though almost enjoyable at times, recording my memoir has been a burden yet a relief as we have spent many hours of recalling in detail my story about the cause and effects of combat on the human spirit. We both agree that if it helps others who are suffering from PTSD, it will be worth all the effort we've put into it. I love my wife and will always appreciate her efforts and participation in writing and bringing to light the story of my never-ending war.

In addition, without the help, encouragement, and support of my friends and fellow marines, this project would have never been completed. My greatest appreciation is to Col. Paul B. Goodwin (USMC Ret.), Lt. Col. Ollie North (USMC Ret.), Major Gen. Tom Braaten (USMC Ret.), John C. Fowler, (Ph. D. CDR/MSC/USN/RET), Ronda Smith (our webmaster and computer assistant), Marsha Fishbaugh, Betty Cundy, and her writing group, along with my brother, Bob. Special thanks to my family—Mike, Eric, Cathy, Teresa, Cynthia, Jill, and Amber—for their encouragement, love, and prayers. Thanks to my dad for his prayers to a loving God who enabled me to come back home and share this story about my favorite heroes in combat that few people have ever heard of before. It has been an honor to know and serve with them.

Introduction

Scars from the meat grinder of Vietnam (PTSD)

A grinder—(a) something that grinds, crushes, or pulverizes by a continual grinding action.

A Mechanical Meat Grinder

When a victim of a meat-grinder accident is fortunate enough to survive the ordeal, it is safe to say they are never physically or emotionally the same again. The near death event becomes a defining moment in the life of the individual forevermore. Each time, they innocently walk into a grocery store meat market, it is highly probable they will experience a flashback to their nightmarish horror of being ripped apart by the excruciatingly, painful incident. The sounds of the processing machines and scent of freshly cut up and grounded meat permeates the air and causes the memory sensors to recall the terrible account, ultimately producing an adrenaline-induced panic attack. They will find themselves having to exit quickly, away from the source of their seizure as they remember the pain and despair associated with the injury. The victim will suddenly discover they are engulfed in a fight or flight mode as they remember the months and even years of enduring agony while recuperating from their wounds. Their lives have been altered and drastically changed in a negative way by the event they were unwittingly subjected to.

A Type of Meat-Grinder Incident

I was a witness to a gruesome meat-grinder incident which happened on a battlefield in Vietnam 1969. The situation was that during a firefight, a North Vietnamese soldier dove beneath an American M48 battle tank in hopes of blowing it up. The quick-thinking driver of the steel behemoth caused the tank to spin in a circle by manipulating the driving tracks in different directions. In a matter of seconds, the dead, mutilated lump of human flesh came shooting out from underneath the back of the tank. His legs, feet, arms, and torso became a heap of undistinguishable flesh and bones. The event was seen as a horrendous way to die even to the most hardened combat marines. Though we hated our enemy with a passion, we kind of hoped he died a quick death because he had been eaten alive by a nasty meat grinder.

An Area Called the Meat Grinder

The most northern area of South Vietnam was a place where two armies met and fought each other on a daily basis. The battles ranged in size, but they were nevertheless engagements with the enemy where many men suffered and died. The region was renowned for being one of the most combative areas in Vietnam and took on several names in which to identify it on military maps. One of the names it was given was the Northern I Corps. It was recognized as the northern one-third of South Vietnam that ran north from Khe Sanh to the demilitarized zone. Most areas north of Khe Sanh were considered free fire zones where if it moved and it wasn't American, ARVN (Army of the Republic of Vietnam), or civilian, we could shoot it with *no* questions asked!

A Country Divided

The demilitarized zone (DMZ) was a four-mile wide buffer of land that ran the width of the country along the seventeenth parallel that separated North and South Vietnam. It was where the North Vietnamese Army (NVA) entered into the southern half of the country to engage those who were fighting for their independence and freedom.

The DMZ became a staging area for the Communist North to mount their forces in an effort to attack and destroy the American-backed South. On any given day, there could be a thousand or more of NVA troops gathering on the northern side of the DMZ border. Firefights, artillery, mortar, and rocket attacks were the norm for most days in the Northern I Corps area. It was an ongoing battle that never seemed to have an end.

On numerous occasions where a cease-fire was called for both sides, many isolated small units of NVA never got the word to stand down and take a break. Knowing this, the Americans could never let their guard down. The constant intensity of the daily grind along the DMZ border caused the area to receive another name that the marine grunts came to know as the meat grinder. A fitting description because of the brutal fighting that took place in the northern provinces of South Vietnam with the North Vietnamese Army.

The Effects of Living in a Meat-Grinder Area

It didn't take long for a fresh brand-new grunt (BNG) to become a hardened warrior that gave no quarter to the enemy. They simply watched and followed the example that was set before them by the experienced veterans leading them. The dead NVA soldiers were left to rot in a bomb crater or just lying out on the open ground. We never buried anyone, and soon, the stench of rotting flesh didn't seem to bother me any longer. We would take pictures of us standing over the dead enemy combatants in a victor's pose because it was a good thing to kill an enemy soldier, just like it would be good to kill a venomous rattlesnake. We made sure he would never hurt or kill anyone again. After every battle, we walked around the area to view the damage done and relish the war-zone scene we had obligingly created. We became almost sociopathic in nature as we learned to kill or be killed and do so without crying or grieving for our own losses. We knew there would be plenty of time for that during the remainder of our lives.

It eventually came to a point in time that it was not only our job to slay the enemy, but it became a pleasure to do so as many of our friends were being hurt and killed almost daily. It doesn't take many firefights to change a person's mind about death and dying as it becomes your primary ambition to kill the enemy. This place was truly a meat-grinder that was causing us to become as complacent as the corner butcher working on a fresh piece of beef. We didn't realize how we were being emotionally changed by the continual grinding that came from living in a deadly killing field as our minds were also unconsciously referencing every event we saw and participated in. At some later date in our lives, a smell, odor, scent, word, or action would bring the traumatic event back to our memory in an amazingly accurate account. There would be *no* escaping our past in the future.

Young, brand new grunts lost our innocence in Vietnam where we found that war was a nasty, dirty business that left its practitioners either physically dead or numbly insensitive to the death that was all around us. There was no such thing as a non-casuality in the meat-grinder of Vietnam. We also found out that there is no dignity in death on a battlefield. Regardless of how tough they are, most soldiers that are killed in battle die violently and scared as they cry out for their mama. As their bodies relax in death, their bowels naturally break lose adding to the degradation and humiliation of dying. Seeing your friends in that condition only adds to your anger and resolve to kill the enemy. By nature, if a callus is formed by continuous friction or rubbing, then we were becoming emotionally calloused. There came a point in time where if one of my friends were killed in battle, they suddenly became a lifeless, colorless, wax-like shell that just ceased to exist. It was like they had never been alive and all they had ever done outside of combat really didn't matter. When realizing this, it became clear to me that I was beginning to go emotionally numb, but it was okay because most of my friends were the same way. We had to become insensitive to death and suffering in order to continue doing our job of killing the enemy amidst losing many men ourselves. It was part of our mental adapting to the destruction of war. The attitude of mental hardness would come back to haunt us later in life as it turned out to be a large component in our never-ending war. I, like many others with PTSD, have tried by my own strength to move on away from the images of war we were exposed to in Vietnam. I've since realized that only through the help of a merciful God, the V.A., and my family, a normal life may be possible for me and all those who have spent time in the grips of an emotional meat grinder.

Though we may not talk about the traumatic events of combat or even bring up the subject in a conversation, we are still plagued by the memories, nightmares, and flashbacks of our experience in Vietnam. The damaging effects of the all-consuming meat-grinder in Vietnam is undoubtedly the reason for our ongoing never-ending war (PTSD).

I've often wondered what my life would be like now if I had known and served God in my youth, instead of going my own way.

> Remember now thy Creator in the days of thy youth, while the evil days come not, nor the years draw nigh, when thou shalt say, I have no pleasure in them (Ecclesiastes 12:1, KJV).

—Ray Clark

A Note from the Author

Because of the subject matter and violent nature of this narrative, the language of combat has been somewhat sanitized in order to make Ray's story easier to read and beneficial to everyone victimized by PTSD. There are many people worldwide who have endured horrific and traumatic events that have forced them to isolate from their family and society, causing them to silently suffer alone. This book is for them, their families, and their friends. I felt that strong, abrasive language or sexual content would be counter-productive and hinder many from reading the entirety of the book. It all must be read in order to glean helpful information about the cause, effect, and treatment of PTSD.

—Laura Clark

Prologue

Not all scars are visible

This is a story about the men of Kilo Company, Third Battalion, Third Regiment, Third Marine Division operating in the most northern area of South Vietnam 1969. The stories in this narrative are based on my perspective as one of the many grunts in Kilo Company. The goal of this account is not to glorify the tragedy of war in any way but to highlight the mental damage incurred through daily surviving in the bush of Vietnam while fighting the North Vietnamese Army in the wilds of a third-world country. *The Never-Ending War* paints a graphic portrait of what deadly combat does to the human spirit and what post-traumatic stress disorder looks like through the eyes of a patient with severe combat-related PTSD. This book gives an exclusive look into the life of America's fighting men on the battlefield as they were being systematically villainized by a hostile homeland that waned in support for its military toward the end of the conflict. The stress of being distanced by their own countrymen merely added unwarranted guilt and grief on the returning veterans as they attempted to reenter society.

Unknown to many Americans at the time, Vietnam had become the kind of war where no one returned home unscathed. Everyone who went there was wounded either physically or emotionally and, for the most part, both. It has also been noted in history as the only war America ever lost. That statement alone creates a gaping wound in the heart of all who went there to fight, leaving no resolve to heal the damage incurred.

Unseen Wounds

Visible wounds are easiest treated because they can be monitored and nursed until fully healed. Soldiers on the battlefield receive the best of care possible for their injury and are awarded a Purple Heart Medal, giving them acknowledgement for their sacrifice from their fellow countrymen. Emotional wounds are a bit different as they can be deeply seated and extremely hurtful, causing agonizing pain that can last a lifetime. The hypersensitive impairments are rarely completely healed because they are constantly being reopened by the daily reminders of the traumatic events along with knowing they were sent to fight a war they were not allowed to win.

The average infantryman in Vietnam could have some type of contact with the enemy 275 out of their 365 days tour of duty. Unbeknown to them, the mental and physical strain of constantly staying alert and being hyper-vigilant would have long term effects on their nervous and adrenal systems. The permanent consequences of being in deadly combat for such a long time would cause them to suffer panic attacks for possibly the remainder of their lives. We all thought the fear and danger would be over when we came back home to live out our lives in peace, but that was not to be the case. There are a myriad of everyday occurrences (or triggers) that cause our adrenaline to rush, ultimately causing unwanted panic attacks. They range from loud noises or crowds of people to strong winds blowing, recreating the chaos of combat. Many combat veterans tend to live in denial and suffer in silence because they don't know how to communicate what they are feeling with those who have not been there. They try to self-medicate with alcohol and drugs to numb their agony, but they only end up worsening their problems with substance abuse and ultimately compounding the pain in their never-ending war. This book is not just another combat narrative. It is much more about the enduring effects of combat on the individual as the reader watches a young marine go from being an innocent, morals-led American teenager into becoming a hardened combat veteran who is forced by survival to break all the rules he was ever taught at home and Sunday school. The guilt and shame of surviving the killing fields of Vietnam would be contributing factors in his own never-ending war. The subject of unjustified guilt is also addressed in the chapter titled Coping Skills. I endeavor to point the reader into the direction of positive help so they can obtain a happy and fulfilled life for themselves and their families. It is God's will that we be at peace with him and ourselves, and he wants to help us achieve that. It has become my passion to share with other victims of PTSD how a loving God has saved, forgiven, and kept me through days when I couldn't help myself—how a devoted family has supported and stood by me when they didn't fully understand PTSD and how the Veterans Administration came by my side when I needed them the most. The final three chapters of this book are dedicated to my personal struggle with adrenaline-induced panic attacks caused by PTSD. I also included the coping skills I used in my daily battle with nightmares, memories, and flashbacks of combat in Vietnam 1969. Through *The Never-Ending War*, I hope to pass on the message that healing and forgiveness can be obtained if the veteran truly wants it. I know this because I've received and experienced it for myself.

—Ray Clark

Bubba! One in Every Crowd

The hours of waiting for a nighttime battle to commence has got to be the most gut-wrenching times ever. Death seemed to be in the air as the Grim Reaper stands by waiting to claim the fallen. The jungle was home to your enemy, and by dusk, he had already left his hiding place to stalk his prey. He moved like a hungry tiger, seeking whom he may devour, searching for the least suspecting victims until he pounces, ripping the life right out of them. In the demilitarized zone (DMZ) of Vietnam, there were no heroes, just scared men who have a job to do. Kill the adversary before he kills you. Tonight, we were sitting in our fighting holes, waiting for the enemy to come and find us as we prepare ourselves to meet and destroy him on his own ground. There would be no smoking or sleeping until the battle was over and the enemy was dead. Then we could rest again.

As the sun sets, a deep, thick darkness engulfs the marines of Kilo Company 3/3/3. Intelligence reports showed that a regiment of North Vietnamese numbering close to two thousand men have been amassing in the area around Mutter's Ridge, and we'd been sent in to find out why. Along with the cloud cover that had blocked any light from the moon, the heavy jungle vegetation, called triple canopy, had caused it to become pitch dark, cutting our visibility to near zero. The blackness of night coupled with a "living, breathing" tropical rainforest seemed to amplify the sounds of the jungle as we could hear things moving all around us on the jungle floor, but we couldn't know who or what was making the noise. It's amazing how noisy a living jungle could be at night when you don't want it to be. We could only imagine the enemy slipping up on us in the darkness, which added to the stress we were already feeling.

An Unseen Enemy

Although we knew there were thousands of enemy soldiers in the vicinity, we still had no way of telling exactly where they were. They, on the other hand, knew our location and would be probing our lines in the darkness, trying to find a weak spot in our flimsy perimeter to attack us. Everyone was unnerved at the idea of a nighttime fight to the death as we strained our eyes and ears, trying to detect anything moving out in front of us. As a usual precaution, we would depend on our trip flares we had set out earlier in the day to light up and expose the approaching enemy troops. The one hundred thousand candlelight flares were set up close to the ground with a twenty-foot long trip wire attached to it. The enemy would accidentally trip on the wire and activate the flare. They were usually very effective in defending a jungle perimeter, making the flares our first line of defense. The NVA knew we used illumination to spread around our perimeter nightly, so they would slowly and methodically crawl around in the darkness, feeling for our trip wires. Once they found one and cut it, the warning device would be rendered useless. They would then have an opening in our lines to attack us.

A Waiting Game

While sitting in the darkness, our gut feeling told us that the North Vietnamese were close by, and they were getting ready to hit us. We couldn't help but wonder about the possible losses we could incur before sunrise as the clock ticked away.

I began to recall an incident that happened to my brother, Bob, who had also been a marine in Vietnam. In 1965, his company was overrun by a North Vietnamese Battalion, and only he and a few other wounded marines were medevaced out before the slaughter took place. The entire marine company was wiped out. With the overwhelming odds against us tonight, it could happen again.

As we continued to stare out into the blackness, Pfc. Hamm burst out with a muffled shout of hostility saying, "Man, I can't stand this waiting! It's killing me!" The sheer dread and terror of what we were expecting to happen before dawn was beginning to take a toll on our nerves. Our clothes were soaked and dripping with sweat as the temperature was still hovering in the low nineties, but we also knew our sweating was not from the heat alone. Our bodies were reacting to the stress we were feeling as death was all around us. We tried to stay calm and quietly reassure each other that as soon as the shooting started, the battle itself would give us plenty of illumination to fight by.

A Strange Anomaly Takes Place

As the tension of battle continued to mount, we began to realize that the overwhelming fear that had been trying to grip us started to diminish as we went from dread to anticipation. We found out that in the final moments before a battle begins, a combatant can get to a point where he is no longer afraid to die. He becomes so focused on killing the enemy that he forgets how scared he is of dying. A great peace comes over him, and he simply gets mad. That's when he is ready to fight. We became so pumped up that we didn't even consider the idea of letting our friends down in battle. We found ourselves getting mad and actually wanting the fight to go ahead and begin. Oorah! The Japanese, Chinese, North Koreans, and North Vietnamese thought it was an honor to die for their country. That's what made them so hard to fight. They attempted to face death with a seemingly unstoppable boldness, and apparently, we were feeling the same kind of rush that they must have been experiencing. Among all those who go to war, very few ever feel the kind of emotional stimulation that deadly combat gives to warriors. That type of adrenaline rush has proved to be one of the major factors in our never-ending war of PTSD.

Help Arrives

Some time during the night, we began to hear the propeller-driven engines of a low-flying aircraft breaking the silence as they circled the ridgeline. We'd heard that sound many times before, and it was always comforting to the grunts to know they were up there watching over us. The aircraft was humorously called Puff the Magic Dragon—a fire-breathing monster.

It was an air force AC47 cargo plane, carrying three mini-Gatling guns that fired three thousand rounds per minute, each. They could cover a football field with one pass-over, placing a bullet in every square foot.

The lumbering old aircraft looked so innocent by its disguise, but what a punch it packed with its super fast machine guns. Every fifth round they fired was a phosphorus-tipped tracer that ignited en route to its target, showing the gunners where the bullets were hitting. It was like a perforated line of red-tipped bullets coming out of the aircraft and heading toward its target. Between each red dot we could see were four .30 caliber rounds we couldn't see. It was an awesome sight to watch.

For the next hour or so, they continued prowling the ridge line and surrounding areas, looking for enemy troops or vehicles that dared to expose themselves.

A short time later, the clouds opened up, and the moon popped out, exposing the gunship flying about two thousand feet above us. It was a godsend as they were dropping flares to help them see any movement below, which also gave us a momentary look at the terrain around us.

Then It Happened

Suddenly, without warning, a single rifle shot rang out, splitting the silence. It sounded like a Soviet-made AK47 that was only a hundred yards or so from our company's position. Was someone actually trying to shoot Puff down with a rifle? Did he not know who Puff was and what he was capable of doing? Did he not think the gunship would see his muzzle flash from the rifle and respond? This guy had to be a complete moron!

Pfcs Renfro, Hamm, and I whispered jokingly as we imagined a scenario of a large number of NVA troops quietly moving through the jungle and possibly setting up to attack us. Suddenly, this idiot decides to impress his friends by shooting down the American airplane. It was like a redneck's famous last words: "Watch this, Bubba." We could just imagine his comrades immediately grabbing hold of him and shaking him roughly and asking, "What did you just do?" Puff instantly responded back by firing two of his three Gatling guns. He distributed a wall of .30 caliber ammunition into a couple acres of jungle from where the rifle shot had come. The imposing army never had time to run as they died where they stood. It was a massacre. Regardless of what the real situation for the enemy had been, it turned into a beautiful light show that Puff was putting on at the cost of the NVA. It was raining death from above, and we were glad he was on our side. We quietly cheered for Puff as some of our tension and stress subsided. A lot of enemy combatants had been eliminated in a matter of minutes, and we didn't have to pull a trigger. We concluded that only God could have pulled this thing off with such ease. Thank the Lord!

The night was still young, and we couldn't let our guard down for obvious reasons. We could rest a little easier in knowing that there were a lot of dead enemy soldiers lying out in the jungle because some moron had decided to slap a dragon named Puff. We'll never know what the rifle shot was really about or how things would have turned out if Puff hadn't showed up. We only knew the mysterious shooter had given his unit's position away and the results that followed. The jungle was quiet for the rest of the night, and the NVA suspended their activity to keep from taking more losses. It was like God had helped us by stopping a nighttime battle before it ever got started. This kind of situation and result was a rarity in the battle with the NVA because they did not usually make this kind of blunder when they were preparing to attack our lines. What had started out to be a simple mistake for them ended up being a major error in judgment that had cost them dearly. All we had to do now was wait through the next few hours of pitch darkness for the sun to finally come up over the horizon and start a new day in the meat grinder for the men of Kilo Company.

Oorah!

Regardless of the normal hype of being tough marines, we were just glad we'd made it through another night on Mutter's Ridge. It seemed like every day up here was just another day in this death trap where somebody you knew was going to get hurt or killed before the day was over. No matter how cautious we tried to be, we could always count on an ambush or mortar attack to open fire on us at any moment. We always tried to stay watchful to danger, but the whole time, we were wondering who would be the next one to get hit. The only word to describe a place like this was *intense* as we stayed keyed up all the time while patrolling the southern edge of the DMZ. The unusually high stress level we were forced to endure in the meat-grinder was constantly recording memories and emotions in our minds that would later return to us and become part of our never-ending war, PTSD.

Even though we were two hundred heavily armed, trained, and motivated United States Marines, we still felt very small up there by ourselves. We knew we were surrounded by a regiment of approximately 1,800 of hardcore NVA soldiers, and this was their backyard. The fear of knowing that in itself was enough to bring on a heart attack, if we allowed it to.

Intercessory Support

I'm sure my dad was always praying for my protection, but the events of tonight were truly amazing. I would write and let him know about the miracle on the ridgeline and ask him to keep praying for us. We needed all the help we could get.

Heading to Vietnam

January 22, 1969. The flight from El Toro, California, to Vietnam had a thirty-minute layover in beautiful Hawaii. As soon as the plane stopped on the tarmac in Oahu, we were marched from the aircraft into a fenced in area where we waited for the plane to be serviced. By the looks of the scenery around us, we couldn't tell this airport from any other we'd ever been in. The only tropical island beauty we saw was contained in the five minutes of landing and taking off again over the islands below. Big deal! Our next destination would be Okinawa, Japan. From there, we'd be heading toward the war-torn country of Vietnam. I'd only seen the destruction and devastation on television where armies were fighting and killing each other, and soon, I'd be part of that war.

The fear of going into deadly combat began to grip me as I wondered about my freezing up with fear in battle or my recognizing who the enemy was and how would it be to kill another human being. I'd read that only fifteen percent of Americans who go to war ever see actual combat. I was now joining the ranks of an elite band of brothers. Fighting the enemy face-to-face is different from anything a man will ever do in his lifetime, and I would soon be doing that very thing. It was fearful and exciting at the same time. It seemed like the longer I sat there and contemplated all the scenarios my imagination could conjure up, the more stressed out I was becoming. I finally took a deep breath and exhaled as my mind began to clear. After working myself into a frenzy over nothing, I suddenly remembered a childhood Sunday School lesson that said most things we imagine will happen never really do. The Marine Corps would, as usual, take care of everything for me, and I would just have to follow orders without question. With that thought in mind, I started to calm down and relax. The only thing to do from here on was to try and make it through the next 365-plus days without getting myself killed. It hadn't seemed like such an ominous task ahead of me until now as we flew into the unknown. My twelve-month tour of duty hadn't started yet and wouldn't until I set foot on Vietnam soil, whenever that would be.

Similar thoughts must have been on the minds of everyone on the airplane because it got really quiet as we flew closer to the coastline of Vietnam. From this point on in our journey, there wasn't much to talk or joke about among ourselves because we didn't know if we even had a future. We all seemed gravely conscious of the fact that our lives were getting ready to be changed throughout the next twelve months. One thing we never anticipated was the long-term detrimental effects that were already being set into motion as we slowly progressed forward into the beginning of our own never-ending war.

Reflecting Back

In the quietness of the flight, I began to look back in time as to how I'd gotten to this point in my life. My journey to Vietnam had started two and a half years earlier. In 1966, I was seventeen years old, was laid off from my job and had recently broken up with my girl friend. Having nothing better to do, I asked my dad if he would sign for me to join the Marine Corps. He reluctantly agreed to let me enlist, knowing that I'd probably get drafted anyway. At least with the marines, I'd be going with the best. That's what the marine recruiter had told us.

Since my induction to the corps on September 23, 1966, I'd spent eight weeks at Parris Island, four weeks at advanced infantry training at Camp Geiger, North Carolina, and the rest of the time standing guard duty at the National Security Agency, Fort Meade, Maryland.

Just before graduation from Parris Island, I was assigned to NSA. I had no idea at the time I'd be there for the remainder of my enlistment in the Marine Corps. Being stationed at Fort Meade for the rest of my four-year commitment was mandatory for the duty station but not the ideal situation for me. I didn't join the Marine Corps to stand guard on a two-by-three foot door mat, monitoring color coded ID badges for the next three and a half years. I joined to be a grunt, marine infantryman, doing what grunts do—fight! It was not that I was a tough guy by any means, but that's what I'd always heard marines do. They're the first to go in and the toughest to fight. My buddies at Fort Meade couldn't understand why I wanted to go to Vietnam, and I couldn't understand why they didn't want to go. For me, this was a once in a lifetime adventure, and I didn't want to miss out on it. What was I thinking?

After a year and a half of constantly requesting to be transfered to WESTPAC (Vietnam), my transfer and reassignment was finally granted. The government had spent a lot of money on my security clearance to get me to the NSA, but in the end, the corps finally allowed me to go to Vietnam in November 1968. I couldn't have been happier. I was granted a fifteen-day leave to spend time with my family before heading to Vietnam. After spending two weeks at home saying good-bye to my dad and little brother, I left for two weeks of training at Camp Pendleton, California, in harsh desert terrain that was nothing like Vietnam. After that, we boarded a Pan American commercial airliner in El Toro, California, bound for Okinawa, Japan. Okinawa was a staging area for troops going to and coming from Vietnam. We landed on Okinawa and trucked to the windward side of the island base where we remained on standby until being cleared to leave for Vietnam. During our time there, we were under strict rules that kept us from leaving the base for any reason. We had to stay close by our barracks in case our unit suddenly received orders to pull out. We didn't want to miss that formation as it could end up costing us a couple of years in a federal penitentiary for being absent without leave (AWOL). Fortunately for us, there were several clubs on base that we could go to after the evening roll call that helped us pass the time away.

The Marine Corps funded club nearest our quarters was called the animal pit, a fitting name for a place where only grunts went to relax. The establishment had a bad reputation for brawls, but it didn't seem to stop anyone from going there as it was always packed out. It opened at 16:30 and closed at 02:00. Even though many marines heading to Vietnam were eighteen years old, everyone could drink as much alcohol as they wanted so long as they didn't get out of hand.

For Our Entertainment

Because there were no women in our area of the base, the club brought in about fifty Okinawan volunteer women each night to dance with and give us some supervised female company. The problem was most of them were grandmas in their sixties. The average age of the marines was nineteen, but the age difference didn't seem to matter to anyone because they were all having a good time. The enlisted marines did not seem to care how big or how old the women were because they were enjoying themselves, and there was a female in the room. The women could not leave the dance hall for any reason, so it was harmless fun to the young marines. After being there an hour or so, it came to my chance to close dance with a tiny woman old enough to be my grandmother. As we danced to the music and talked, we stared into each others' eyes. The idea of kissing this silver-haired tropical beauty suddenly came into my mind and as we inched closer to each other. Suddenly, I came to my senses. I thought, *No! What am I thinking? This is like making out with my grandmother.* I couldn't do it. The song soon ended, and I walked her back to her seat. I was

34 ★★★

embarrassed. I returned to the table where my buddies were sitting, laughing raucously at the whole situation.

For the remainder of the night, I gave up trying to force myself on Granny and focused on having a good time with my friends. Granny was probably glad to escape this idiot marine's advances too. This place was a circus and definitely not the kind of USO show we would write home and tell our mothers about. It was unquestionably an animal pit.

At one point during the night, I saw a couple marines fighting over one grandma. The jarheads were scrapping, and the many onlookers were laughing. It was like the old Marine Corps saying: "There are no ugly women after midnight." That wild week in Okinawa would be the last good time I'd have before heading into the meat-grinder of Vietnam for the next twelve months. I should have been seeking God's protection and grace instead of running from him.

Moving Out

In the late morning of February 3, a formation was called, and we were told to grab our gear and fall back in. "We're moving out!" It was really happening, and we were on our way. We went to the airport and boarded a C-130 military aircraft and took off. Our next stop would be Vietnam.

We arrived late that afternoon in Vietnam airspace and were told that we could not land because the DaNang Airbase was getting shelled, and it was not yet safe. We would be circling the base until the attack ended. We were then instructed to disembark the plane as soon as it stopped moving. We had to get away from the aircraft as quickly as possible because it was the target for the incoming rockets.

About this time, the thought hit me: getting shelled. I had never heard those words before. Throughout my time in the Marine Corps, I had always been shooting at targets that didn't shoot back. Now we are just landing in this foreign country, and we are being fired on while we are still trying to land the plane. People down there are possibly being wounded and killed by incoming rockets and mortars, and that's exactly where we're headed. This country was beginning to look more serious and unfriendly by the minute.

Salty Marine

Sitting next to me on the aircraft was a staff sergeant that was also a cook. He told me earlier that this would be his third tour over here. I deliberately sat next to him on the plane because he was an old salt, a time-tested marine, and I was sure he would know what was going on and where I needed to be. I figured if anyone would be cool and calm under pressure, it would be him. While the plane continued our circling pattern, I looked over and saw he was crying like a baby while kissing a St. Christopher medal that was hanging around his neck. I thought maybe this was a good time for me to say a little prayer for me too, so I did. The staff sergeant looked over at me praying and burst out crying even harder. "Good Lord!" This guy was coming apart, and he was not even a grunt. The only thing salty about him was his cooking. As he leaned over to pray, my eyes caught a glimpse of his religious medal hanging around his neck, and suddenly, it began to make sense for me to find a cross, crucifix, or something that represented God as soon as possible. It looked like I'd need all the help I could find in order to get back home again a year from now.

Vietnam

About a half hour later, we were cleared to land, and our wheels finally touched down on Vietnam soil. Great! I was finally here and still alive.

As we disembarked the aircraft, we were hurriedly taken away from the airfield and into some empty barracks nearby. A short time later, the sun went down, and it got real dark. We couldn't have any lights on in the barracks because they would draw enemy rocket or mortar fire from the hills around us, so we sat in the doorway of the building. We were also warned about smoking a cigarette on the outside grounds after dark because snipers were up in the hills surrounding the base. A glowing coal on a cigarette could be seen for over a mile away creating a great target to shoot at. The temperature was over a hundred degrees and made the barracks very hot and musky inside. It was starting to look like it would be a long sleepless night ahead of us. This was my first night in Vietnam, and I was already miserable. I turned in early because there was nothing else to do, and we were too scared to roam around in the darkness, not knowing who or what we might walk into.

First Day in Country

The next morning, we were awakened early and taken to breakfast. Everything was crude looking and covered in thick red dust. Red clay was everywhere, and the Jeeps, tanks, and trucks kept the dust flying and landing on everything around the base. The landscape was parched dry, and it looked like it hadn't rained in a long time. There was no vegetation anywhere on the base because it had to be cleared away for security reasons. I was amazed to see that DaNang had turned out to be a huge city of shanty houses and businesses with a modern American airbase in the middle of it. The base was bustling with the activity of a modern military except for the dust and dirt covering everything.

Being it was all military, most buildings around the airbase were made of canvas. The lower part of the buildings was made of sandbags, and the rest of the way up looked like tents. Some barracks were all wooden with no paint or shiny roofs that would call attention to enemy mortar men. The only living quarters that looked like apartments were the air force barracks. They were said to have had a swimming pool in them. Figures! They took advantage of government funding and got the best of everything. The Marine Corps gave half of the money they got back to the government because the old equipment we were using was good enough for us.

Later that morning, we were taken to an area where we were being assigned to units.

Some marines were going south, and some were going to units in the north. I really hadn't done a lot of homework, so I didn't know if one was any better than the other. I did remember to avoid going to First Battalion Ninth Marines if possible.

I'd heard marine combat veterans at the animal pit warning us to stay away from that unit at all cost. They were called the walking dead because the First Battalion Ninth Marines had done some brutal things to the dead North Vietnamese, like cutting their ears off and making chains with them. The North Vietnamese took this kind of thing very seriously. A regiment of the North Vietnamese Army (NVA) were assigned to attack the marine battalion every time they stopped, and the casualties began mounting. From all the information I'd heard, I really didn't want to be part of the walking dead.

As we lined up to be assigned to our unit, I overheard the guy sitting at the desk say to the two marines in front of me, "One-nine, the walking dead." My heart sank at the thought, and I said a little silent prayer. I was beginning to lose some of my bravery and courage I'd been feeling up to this point. I suddenly thought about my friends at Fort Meade and wondered what they were doing about this time—going to a football game or going out on a date with their girlfriend. War did not seem so glamorous anymore. It started to look dirty and dangerous, and there was a possibility of me getting myself hurt or killed over in this place, and none of my old friends would even know about it. Going to the walking dead made me feel small, alone, and a little frightened at the thought of having to kill people so they would not kill me. It was a very sobering thought.

As I stepped up to the desk, the marine found my name on the roster and said, "You'll be going to K Company, Third Battalion, Third Regiment, Third Marine Division."

I smiled inwardly and said, "Thank you, Lord." It was not 1/9, and that was good enough for me. At the moment, I just didn't know that going to 3/3/3 rather than 1/9/1 was like getting off the *Titanic* and getting onto the Hindenburg. The 3/3/3 was down south at the time on Operation Taylor Common but would soon be going back up north to where some of the heaviest fighting of the war was taking place. That area was called Leatherneck Square because of the massive Marine Corps buildup and presence in that area, which sounded like a pretty good place to go. The next thing I learned threw a damper on the whole situation as I found out that particular region was better known to the marines who fought there as the meat-grinder because of the high amount of casualties on both sides of the war. A meat-grinder. Now that was a name that didn't sound so great!

I soon discovered there were two kinds of wars being fought in South Vietnam. In the southern provinces, the American forces were having to fight the Viet Cong (VC). They were civilian soldiers that looked, acted like and worked civilian jobs by day, and roamed around at night fighting the American and south Vietnamese forces. They were the communist forces behind the Civil War itself. A peasant farmer could be innocently hoeing in a rice paddy, and when you passed by him, he would put down his hoe, pick up a rifle that had been lying beside him, and shoot you in the back. It was said that you couldn't trust anyone down south. The VC also used small children as suicide bombers. The youngsters would have explosives attached to them and be sent into a crowd of Americans or South Vietnamese soldiers with the promise of being given candy by the soldiers. The perpetrators would then at their own time and discretion detonate the bomb.

The Americans down south also had to deal with a lot of booby traps and tunnels in which the Viet Cong soldiers stashed their supplies and arms. If you didn't stay on hyper-alert all the time, the next step you took could be your last one, as the Viet Cong were everywhere.

The Northern I Corps Area

In the northern areas of South Vietnam, the Americans were fighting against the North Vietnamese Army (NVA). It was a regular, formidable army that wore uniforms for the most part and had some Chinese and Russian equipment that was better than ours. They didn't normally shoot and run like the VC were known to do. These guys would stand and fight you head-on. Many times, they would hold their ground until the American air wing would show up. Only then would they take off into the jungle, knowing that if they were caught out in the open, they would be blown to pieces. If at all possible, when the bombs did drop, the NVA would try to run into their bunkers or trenches to avoid the blast, and you would have to start all over again as soon as the jets were gone. These were seasoned veterans of battle, and they didn't give up easily. The northern area of the country had one little advantage over the fighting in the south. It was simply being able to identify the enemy by their uniforms. The Vietnamese had been fighting for over fifty years with the Chinese, Japanese, French, and now, Americans. There were tunnel complexes that ran for hundreds of miles in which they had built large rooms underground that held their hospitals, rest centers, ammunition, and food storage depots.

A marine could walk up on a two feet wide entry hole in the middle of a large open field that would turn out to be much more than just a hole in the ground. A tunnel rat, a small marine, would be sent down into the opening, armed with a pistol and a flashlight, to see what he could find. It might be an arms cache or a hospital with many enemy soldiers in it. The tunnel-rat job was one that no one wanted to do, and most of us avoided being the tunnel rat if at all possible.

An hour or so after finding out my destination, I jumped on the back of a truck, and we headed down the road about five miles to where our battalion headquarters was located. There were several other marines on the truck with me, and I met one named Bob Snyder from Harpers Ferry, Maryland. We became friends and ended up being in the same platoon in Kilo Company. As we crossed a bridge along the way, a shot rang out, and everyone ducked down to the floor of the truck. No one got hit, but the driver told us to keep our heads down, and from then on, we did. We asked when we would get a rifle to shoot back with, and they just replied, "In due time." I thought getting a rifle and ammunition in this place would be a great idea.

The Battalion Rear Area

Once at battalion, we were taken to our company command area and introduced to the officers in charge of Kilo Company's command and logistics center. Everyone there was part of a skeleton crew holding the rear section down while the main company was running search-and-destroy missions farther south, about twenty miles out into the bush. The rear was like a staging area for rotating troops and those who were going to or coming from R&R (rest and recuperation), a seven-day vacation funded by the government.

Looking around the compound, I noticed a lot of marines were filling sandbags that would be used in fortifying the complex. Even though the bags could take a bullet or a piece of shrapnel better than a body could, the marines weren't real happy about filling them while they were supposed to be on vacation. They wanted to rest as much they could before going back out into the bush. They knew they'd be returning to the wilds soon enough.

First Things First

We were first taken to the company armory and issued an M16 rifle. It was the first time I had ever seen one up close, and it looked like a plastic toy. From what I'd heard about the new rifle, it was not the most trusted or dependable weapon in our arsenal, but it was what they gave us to use. The famous weapon was first used extensively in Vietnam as a short, light-weight bush rifle. Even though they were widely accepted at the first, they soon developed a problem with their firing mechanisms, almost making them infamous. Quite a few marines were killed on hills 881 and 861when their newly issued M16 rifles jammed up on them and quit firing in the middle of a major firefight with the NVA. One marine rifleman wrote to his family after the battle: "We left with seventy-two men in our platoon and came back with nineteen."

Practically every one of our dead was found with his M16 torn down next to him, where he had been trying to fix it ("Defense: Under Fire." *Time Magazine*, June 09, 1967.) Through an exhaustive investigation, it was found out to be a problem with the primer on the bullets causing the misfire and not the weapon itself. The rifle was put back into use right away, though the foot soldiers throughout Vietnam always doubted the reliability of the weapon when it was most needed. They looked like they were made of plastic and were humorously called Mattie Mattels because they looked like a toy. The guy at the armory told me to keep it clean, and I'd be all right. We were also given a bandolier of M16 ammunition, ten magazines for our rifle, four grenades, two backpacks, two canteens, a light-weight blanket, jungle fatigues, and anything else they thought we would need out in the Bush.

They then took us over to a target range where we sighted in our rifles at thirty and forty yards. To our surprise, the distance between us and the targets was amazingly close. The rifle coaches told us that from that distance, we could get an idea of how close the enemy would be from us in a firefight. We practiced firing our weapons until we could hit the target every time as we found out the M16 was not a toy. We also fired a M79 grenade launcher that shot explosive rounds. It looked like a fat shotgun that really made a mess when it hit something. We threw a few grenades just for practice so we'd be prepared for the real thing when it came time. We continued target-practicing until we became familiar and confident with our weapons. As we did, we began to feel a little more comfortable and secure with our famous M16 rifle. We would be heading out into the bush in the morning. After getting the remainder of our issued gear, we were taken to a squad-sized tent that held about twelve cots for our sleeping pleasure. The makeshift beds were not comfortable, but at least they kept us off the ground. I might have enjoyed it more if I'd known it would be the last time I would sleep on a cot or in a tent for a long time. Marines like to pack light, no blow-up mattresses or sleeping bags, so they can fight, and we really practiced that rule.

Rest and Relaxation

Once in a twelve-month tour of duty, you could qualify for a seven day R&R to any one of the designated places like Japan, Australia, Singapore, Hong Kong, or even Hawaii. You had to be in the country for six months before you became eligible for R&R, and almost everyone took advantage of it, except for some like me. I made up my mind early into my tour that I'd never take

R&R and blow all my saved-up money on some Asian street girl. They were beautiful enough, but because they looked so much like the ones I was trying to kill, I just didn't want to get too close to them. With my mind-set as it was, I could snap and kill one of them in a moment of drunken rage. My thought was if I make it back home alive, I'll spend my small fortune on some round-eyed American girl back in the States. With the six months stipulation in place, many marines would be seriously injured or killed before they qualified.

Our Second Night

We were now brand-new grunts in Kilo Company. Part of our breaking-in agenda called for Bob Snyder and me to be given a guard duty assignment. We were to walk around several tents in the compound for about two hours, looking for any out of control fires or whatever—basically, fire watch. We knew there were real guards all around the outside perimeter for real security, and they were just giving us something to do because we were new.

We noticed trenches were dug around most tents and buildings in the compound. Before starting our guard watch, we were instructed that if we got rockets or mortars during the night, we were to jump into the trench with our helmet, flak jacket, and rifle. We really didn't know what to think of all this as we just followed orders and kept our mouth shut. As I began walking around the tents, guarding whatever, I came up on a couple guys smoking something that had a distinct odor of marijuana. They asked me if I smoked. Knowing what they meant, I replied sure. They passed me the joint and told me to take a hit. I didn't want to look like a narc or outsider, so not knowing what else to do, I just joined in. Suddenly, the thought of getting caught smoking this stuff on guard duty began to scare me, so I gave it back and refused any more offers. It was just enough connection to get me into a conversation with these veterans of the bush. As we started to talk, they told me that the only time to smoke pot was in the rear area, where it was relatively safe. There is no playing around out in the bush because you had to keep your head straight out there.

As we were standing next to the tent talking and laughing, two explosions suddenly shattered the night's silence. Complete chaos erupted, and someone yelled, "Incoming!" This meant that enemy mortars or rockets were dropping into the compound as everyone nearby jumped into our trench and knelt down to cover up. There were people running everywhere in the darkness and diving into any cover they could find. After a few minutes of silence, someone yelled out, "All clear!" We climbed out of our trenches, and I got back to guarding my tents as everyone else returned to whatever they had been doing before the incident. It seemed exciting! A short time later, we found out that it was not incoming at all. Some disgruntled marine, upset about the sandbag detail, had thrown two grenades into the gunnery sergeant's tent as a warning to lighten up on them or else. The despicable warning to the gunny had also come to me as a clear message that this was the reality of being in a place where everyone is armed and deadly. Making friends over here was not an option, and I didn't need any more enemies than necessary.

I later sat in my tent and pondered on the situation I'd witnessed. Who was the enemy, and who could be trusted? My confidence in our band of brothers was a bit shaken by the anonymous bomber who actually lived among us. The news back home had always talked about racial tensions in Vietnam, but I didn't see any among the marine grunts in the rear area. Troop cohesion was even better out in the bush where everyone got along pretty good. We were constantly being reminded that our common enemy was the NVA. Someone once said that in combat, you don't look at the man's skin color next to you, you just make sure that both of you are pointing your weapons in the same direction. We might have come to this place in different types of ships, but now, we were all in the same boat, trying to make it back home alive. It would take all of us working together to get that accomplished.

While standing outside my tent, a couple old salts came over and asked me if I wanted to sneak out of the compound with them and go into this little village near us. I really appreciated their offer but declined. I'd already heard too many stories in Okinawa about how the NVA would use women to seduce the man while the enemy soldiers would come in and cut his throat. Along with that were the many horrid stories about social diseases. It all kept me from ever wanting to mess with anyone. I had enough to worry about without putting myself at risk like that.

I finally ended my guard shift and was able to hit the sack. It was miserable from the heat inside the tent and the sleeping contraption they called a cot was hard, but it was better than nothing. Lying down was better than standing up, so I took the better of the two. I found it hard to sleep, for I was thinking about going out into the bush the next morning. I wondered how it was going to be out there, hunting for the elusive enemy and hoping he would not find you first. As scary as it was, this was the Marine Corps I had always dreamed of, and now it was really happening. One, I was in the United States Marine Corps. Two, I was a grunt, 0311 Infantry Marine. Three, I was in a heavy combat zone in Vietnam. Four, it couldn't have been any better than this for a young American man. Five, I would forever be glad I'd chosen this path in my younger days. I just hoped that I would be able to do everything they wanted me to do and not end up being responsible for someone getting hurt.

The Bush

On the morning of February fifth, they put us on a CH46 helicopter and headed out to the mountains, nineteen miles southwest of DaNang where Operation Taylor Common was being conducted. The terrain we were flying over was mountainous and covered in different shades of green. A few hills had obviously been occupied before because they had been cleared of all vegetation with fighting holes dotting the perimeter around the top of them. There were also bomb craters on and around several hills in the vicinity that indicated something terrible had happened there at some time or another. Everything was lush and green, and it appeared to be a good place to hide and a terrible place to have to find someone. Even to a new grunt in country, it was easy to guess who would be hiding and who would be seeking in this game of life and death that was already being played out in the jungles below. It became apparent as to how destructive man can be to God's green earth. Man messes up everything he touches. A short time later, we landed and ran out the back of the helicopter toward the nearest fighting hole, not foxhole, we came to. The idea is that army soldiers hide in foxholes, but marines fight in fighting holes. The marines like to point out that there is a great difference. Our chopper quickly took off again, leaving us in a world like I'd never been before. I'd trained for Vietnam in the woods of Camp Lejeune, North Carolina, but this was nothing like the forest with pine trees and thinned-out forest floor. This place was pure jungle where the ground could not even be seen for vegetation. There were no thinned-out areas around our perimeter, and it appeared the enemy could hide within yards of us without ever being seen. Of course, the good part was they couldn't see us either.

We BNG, brand-new grunts, were in a cultural shock and about seventy pounds heavier due to the abundance of equipment we were carrying. Grunts believe that it is better to have something and not need it rather than to need something and not have it.

With that thought in mind, we tried to carry any-and everything we might need in the days to come. The tropical forest we had just landed in would be our new home until we moved to another jungle or mountain hilltop somewhere else.

Life in the Bush

Along with all the equipment we were required to have, we could haul around as much stuff as we were willing to carry, such as the amount of canteens of water or ammunition for our weapons. It was heavy and cumbersome to get used to, but this was just one of the new hurdles we were finding as we joined Kilo Company out in the bush.

One of the first things we learned was how to properly dress for the field. We put our fighting gear on first—flak jacket, bandoliers of ammo, grenades, and one canteen of water. We then added on our backpacks and any other extra gear we didn't necessarily need in a firefight. When something bad happened, we would automatically drop our packs and be ready to go into action in seconds. It all made sense to a bunch of green, inexperienced marines that were eager to find out how to stay alive out in the bush of Vietnam.

The extremely high temperature and humidity was one of the first things we noticed. It was hovering over a hundred degrees with a hot breeze blowing, doing very little to cool things off. The marines had made tents by tying their ponchos to nearby limbs near their fighting holes to bring them a slight degree of relief from the scorching sun. The environment was hot and dirty, but we couldn't complain about anything. Having just arrived here, we didn't have the right to gripe yet. These guys had been out here for two months, and they looked like it. They were ragged and dirty faced with their camouflaged utilities that were sun bleached, and most of them had mustaches and needed a shave. They looked tough and cool at the same time. This was nothing like the Marine Corps I'd been with for the past two and a half years. We were told that water was scarce up on top of the mountain, so they didn't have to shave as much. It also dawned on me that you couldn't take a bath or freshen up out here whenever you felt like it. We couldn't wear deodorant or aftershave because the enemy would pick up the scent and ambush you. The safest thing to do in the wilds was to smell like the wilds. You had to become part of the environment if you wanted to live. The little everyday conveniences we'd always known and enjoyed had no place out here in the bush. For the time being, we'd have to adapt, improvise, and overcome while fighting a third-world country on their soil and by their rules of warfare. There was no hiding our BNG status among our counterparts. Our brand-new camouflaged utilities really stuck out next to the sun-bleached ones everyone else was wearing. They had been wearing the same clothes for the past two months 24-7. Our boots drew attention too by being as black as coal. The longer you were out in the bush, the whiter they became from the beating of the rough terrain. Having worn-out boots was like a right of passage, and everyone knew you had paid your dues by being in the bush for an extended period of time.

We were introduced to our company commander, Captain J. Rapuano; our platoon commander, Second Lieutenant B. Haskell from Upper Marlboro, Maryland; and our platoon sergeant, S/Sgt. Jose Cruz from California. We also met our assistant platoon sergeant Cpl. Tom "Rudi" Rudisill from Michigan. He took us over to meet our squad members as they were coming in from a patrol. Rudi looked like a marine's marine. With his six-foot-tall frame and a muscular build, he seemed to have a natural leadership quality that made everyone want to be like him. There was no doubt he would know what to do when things got tough. He really impressed us from the very beginning as someone you wanted to stay close to. I was first introduced to our squad leader, Corporal Rios. He, in turn, put me in L/Cpl. James Grogan's fire team along with L/Cpl. Gary Kobra and Pfc. Terry Ruggie. Grogan was a stocky, red-headed, and freckled-face marine from Boston, Massachusetts. He had a heavy Boston accent that pronounced most words without an *r* like *car* is *ca*, *bar* is *ba*, and so on. Trying not to be obvious about his strange brogue, it was comical listening to him talk. Kobra and Ruggie were both from Sheboygan, Wisconsin. They had grown up together and entered the Marine Corps on the buddy plan, staying together throughout their four-year enlistment obligation. They were the ones I would work closest to within our squad.

A marine rifle company was made up of three rifle platoons and one weapons platoon (mortar, machine guns, etc.) along with officers, corpsmen, and specialists of different fields. Each rifle platoon was made up of three thirteen-man squads. Each squad was made up of three four-man assault teams plus a squad leader. Each squad could work singularly or corporately with other teams. The entire company was basically an assembly of many four-man assault teams that could act independently if need be, making the company part of a legendary fighting force.

Most of the guys in our squad asked where I am from and what was going on back in the States, We looked at each other's pictures and talked of our wives or girl friends waiting for us back home. One of the guys had a picture of a huge girl lying on a couch. He asked me what I thought of her. I told him that she looked pretty good and then dropped the conversation. It was okay with me if he thought she was the finest chick he had ever known. When talking to some of the others, they asked me if I had seen this guy's girl friend. I didn't answer, but we all laughed and agreed without saying a word. I then wished I'd taken a picture of my silver-haired sweetheart of a dance partner at the animal pit. I wonder what they would have said about my girlfriend.

My New Home Away from Home

I was taken to Kobra and Ruggie's fighting hole where we got ready for the night to close in on us. Nights in the jungle were especially dark and dangerous, shrouding us in a thick blanket of obscurity and making it hard to fight what we couldn't see. We kept our weapons, flak jackets, and helmets in our fighting hole with us and put everything else we had within our reach on the outside of the hole. Most things we were doing had been rehearsed many times in training, but now it was for real. If we messed up in our combat training exercises, it really didn't matter so much as we might get chewed out, but that's about all. If we messed up now, it could cost us our lives. That was a sobering thought. I asked Kobra and Ruggie how they wanted to work our three-man perimeter watch.

We would normally rotate our guard all night, taking turns staying awake for one hour and then wake up the next man for his watch and so on. I was shocked by their answer.

They told me that in their opinion, there were no gooks up on the top of the mountain and there was no need to have a watch. Besides, no one ever checked the perimeter lines anyway. I didn't know what to say or do. This was my first night in the bush, and they were supposed to know what they were doing, regardless of what I thought. I asked Ruggie, "What happens if we get caught?" He assured me that he'd say, "It was his turn to watch," and with that said, we went to sleep as I wondered if we'd all wake up dead.

Just before sunrise, we were awakened out of a sound sleep with someone barking, "Who's supposed to be on watch?" No one said a word. They asked again, "Who's on watch here?" I looked at Ruggie and Kobra as they both just stared back at me.

Being the new guy, it seemed only reasonable to take the responsibility. I replied back, "It must be me, sir." It was Lieutenant Haskell and Corporal Rudisill glaring at us with contempt in their eyes. I really hated for them to think I'd jeopardized everyone's lives by going to sleep on watch, but I didn't know what else to do. Haskell told me to stay awake, and he'd take care of me later. I said, "Yes, sir," and then they left. Both Kobra and Ruggie thanked and assured me they would help with my punishment detail. I thought, *Yeah, right!*

I'd learned two lessons on my first night in the Bush—one, don't fall asleep on watch, and two, don't fall for some stupid idea like that again. Operation Taylor Common ended a short time later and was accessed as a complete success. The marines had killed 171 enemy soldiers and captured seven. The multi-unit operation had swept and cleared a lot of territory around the An Hoa basin and surrounding mountains. The US Army, Marine, and South Vietnamese Army units had destroyed many enemy base camps, staging areas, and supply depots. Some of the food and medical supplies confiscated had stickers on them saying, "Donated by a well-known American university." Everyone knew that it was part of the psychological warfare the NVA was using on us, but they also knew it was true. This same university was sending money to our enemy for food and medical supplies, but instead, the NVA were using the donations to buy anything they needed to fight us with. Some of the men just blew it off like they didn't care while others took it personally. I took it personally.

Operation Taylor Common Ends

We were choppered off the mountain a couple days later and were flown back to DaNang, The operation had ended, and we were heading back up north to the DMZ (demilitarized zone), an invisible line that ran the width of the country, dividing the North, Communists, from the South, freedom fighters.

The way everyone was talking, it didn't sound like a good move. Nevertheless, we were going anyway, whether we liked it or not.

We landed in DaNang around noon with the scorching temperature hovering over a hundred degrees. There was no shade in the area for us to take shelter, so we took our steel helmets off and put on our soft utility covers to get a little reprieve from the blistering sunshine. Because the battalion had been out in the bush for over sixty days, someone sent out a jeep, pulling a trailer full of ice-cold beer. Normally, everyone would have jumped on the wagon and downed all the beer they could hold, but it was exceptionally hot out in the sunshine. Without knowing what our schedule would be, we naturally figured we'd be at DaNang for a few days before moving north, and we could get drunk later when it cooled off. Apparently, not everyone thought that way because a couple of the guys started drinking beers as fast as they could. One even lay down in a mud puddle and started splashing around as he drank his fill of the golden nectar.

Some of the local POGs, (people other than grunts), came out of their living quarters and stared at us like we were from another planet. They were clean from head to toe, and we looked like a bunch of bandit marauders compared to them. We kind of liked looking like that because they seemed to be scared of us. No one would have ever thought we were in the same Marine Corps.

A short time later, we marched off to a mess hall where they served us steak and baked potatoes. It was really good and a whole lot better than the usual C rations we ate every day.

The local marines at the base didn't seem to be real friendly to a bunch of grunts coming off of a long operation. They thought we were like a horde of nomads, intending to vandalize and steal everything we could get our hands on. They didn't know the only thing we wanted from anyone was food stuff (hot sauce, onions, etc.), and that came from the mess halls. We didn't want their toys or electronic gadgets because we would have to carry them, and we had plenty to haul around as it was. Besides, we couldn't have the distractions of radios out in the bush with us anyway.

The POGs around us were always easy to spot. They were always taking pictures of each other in starched utility uniforms, spit-shined boots, and an array of weapons. They would have a machine gun in each hand, two bandoliers of machine gun ammunition strapped across their chest, a pistol on each hip, several grenades hanging from their flak jacket, and several knives strapped to their ankle, leg, hip, and arm. In all probability, the only fight they ever got into was at a local bar, and they more than likely lost that one. The Veterans Administration accessed that only about fifteen percent of those who went to Vietnam ever saw sustained combat, and they were mostly grunts. Everyone wanted to look like a grunt, but nobody wanted to go outside their safe compound to become one. I loved being a marine grunt in a combat zone. That was the coolest thing anyone could ever do.

The Awkward Flight North

After we finished eating our fill of steak dinner, we were rounded up by platoons and unexpectedly marched to the nearby airfield. The heat was still sweltering when they herded us into a C130 cargo plane that held the whole platoon of forty men as long as you didn't use the pull-down seats along the sides of the aircraft. We walked in and packed up as close to the men around us as possible. They closed the back ramp and said, "Sit down." We squirmed our way to the floor and got situated. As our flight sat waiting on the airport tarmac, things began heating up. We had thought it was hot outside, but now we were shut up inside the airplane. The temperature must have gotten to 130 degrees while we were waiting to take off. There was no breeze at all, and we felt like we were roasting inside an oven. We began sweating profusely, and it even became difficult for us to breathe inside the blistering-hot cabin.

As we sat there with sweat dripping off of us, I noticed the marine directly in front of me, Lance Corporal Pepper, was starting to get sick. He was the one who had gotten drunk and gone swimming in the mud puddle a short time ago. Now he was full of steak and baked potato, getting hotter and sicker by the minute. Everyone near him started to inch away as far as they could as it became evident what was about to happen. He looked around for a place to barf, but there was no place to go. We were sitting on top of our packs and squeezed together as close as we could get to each other. Everyone close to him started panicking and telling him that he had better not throw up on them. He didn't hear a word they said. He looked to his left and then to his right, and all of a sudden, here it came. It was like a geyser blowing off right into the guy's left ear next to him. The one he threw up on, Corporal Dalson, never moved. He must have been in shock because he just sat there while Pepper let go two more times into his ear, running down onto and into his camouflaged utility jacket. When Pepper momentarily stopped after the third belch, Dalson turned and looked at him. He didn't say a word. He just stared at him with his teeth clenched and his eyes glaring in a look of total disdain. Pepper looked down at the floor and saw a flimsy, soft utility cap lying there and picked it up. He started to wipe Dalson's ear out as best he could with the cover, trying to somehow ease the damage he'd done to Dalson's pride and self-esteem. The humiliated and embittered Dalson mumbled out a few almost undistinguishable words as he asked him, "Who's soft cover are you using?" Pepper looked inside the brim and saw the name "Dalson." He mumbled softly, "Yours."

Dalson looked like he was going to explode. He pointed at the rear gate of the airplane and said, "When that door opens, you're a dead man." L/Cpl. Bill Bushey picked up Pepper's helmet that was sitting on the floor next to him and said, "Throw up in that, stupid!" It was all we could do to keep from bursting out laughing. Everyone around them was quietly shaking and trembling from watching the most disgusting comedy show we'd ever seen. No one laughed or said a word until after we had landed. It could have happened to anyone, but I was glad it wasn't me in the melee.

Pepper threw up a couple more times while in flight, but he used his helmet instead of Dalson's ear. The sight and stench of his throw-up filled the aircraft and just about brought others to the verge of getting sick themselves. Fortunately, no one else did. We finally landed at Dong Ha airbase about an hour or so later, and as we were getting off the plane, an officer standing by the rear gate saw Pepper carrying his helmet in his hand instead of wearing it. He ordered him to put it on. Dong Ha was a combat base in the Northern I Corps area, and everyone had to wear their helmet at all times. Pepper tried to explain to the officer about getting sick during the flight, but the captain cut him off and said, "Get that helmet on, Marine!" Pepper abruptly put the helmet on and walked off with throw-up dripping off the sides of his head.

This had to be one of the worst days of Pepper's and Dalson's lives. I was so glad I didn't drink any beer that day because I was a new guy, and I, like Pepper, would have never lived it down. This is probably one war story that Pepper and Dalson would never tell their families. They would rather forget it ever happened.

C-2 Artillery Base

After being at Dong Ha Airbase for a few short hours, we were trucked to a forward US Army Artillery Base called Compound-2. It was located in the Northern I Corps area of Vietnam known as Leatherneck Square. A name derived from the Third Marine Division occupying a large part of the northern one-third of the country.

The base was only a couple of miles from the demilitarized zone, making it an easy target for the NVA to fire rockets into the compound every morning and afternoon just like clockwork.

Even though the base was operated by the US Army, the outer perimeter had to be secured by a full company of marines all the time. One of the four companies in our battalion—India, Kilo, Lima, or Mike—would take their turn securing the base while the other three companies were running patrols in the meat grinder. While performing security duties for the base, we would take a break from living in the bush while being refitted with supplies and replacement marines (BNGs).

In front of the marine's defensive line positions and bunkers were several strands of barbed and rolled wire surrounding the base along with thousands of land mines planted to protect the compound from invaders. There was only one road running through the base in order to provide maximum security from having multiple-entry points. Every precaution was taken to keep the most northern artillery base from ever falling into enemy hands. One of the problems with properly defending the base was due to it being so large and the marines so few. A full marine company consisted of approximately two hundred men, but Kilo Company generally ran around 180 or so. There were always men leaving our company because of combat casualties, R&R stints, or rotation back to the states. The difficulty with security came from having a smaller number of men to use on line watch, creating huge gaps, fifty yards or so, between the marine's fighting positions. We hoped we'd never get attacked by a large force of NVA because it would be almost impossible to keep the adversary from breaching the lines, especially if the army was lying about land mines being there. They were our first line of defense.

On our third day there, I received word that Lieutenant Haskell wanted to see me ASAP.

Hoping that he'd forgotten about my sleeping incident, it suddenly dawned on me that he hadn't. I then immediately and reluctantly reported to him at the command bunker. He told me to go with Pfc. Frank "Indian" Eullo on a working party he had picked especially for me. Indian was going to instruct me in the art of burning outhouse waste. I had no idea of what were they talking about, and by the way everyone was laughing, I had no desire to find out. The chief was in trouble again, and apparently, this was not his first time with the mission because he was considered the local expert on burning these things. I found out a little while later that our superiors didn't trust just anyone to do the job alone anymore, especially newcomers like me. A guy named Knolls was sent out by himself to do the job and ended up burning the entire outhouse down. After that incident, it became a mandatory two man job.

The way it worked was for us to go to the back of the little five-by-five-foot building and open the doors at the bottom of the shack. Inside were several two-foot high drums with the lids cut off and placed under each toilet seat. They would strategically catch everything coming their way. I pulled the full one out and replaced it with an empty one. I then dragged the full one away from the building, trying not to splash any of the sludge on me. I then poured in diesel fuel mixed with sulfur pellets into the barrel. Indian stirred and set it on fire as we stepped back. We had to remain with it because the sludge had to be stirred periodically to make sure it was burning up completely. We tried to stay away from the smoke because the stench of the burning material permeated the air, our clothing and everything else it touched. This was a nastiest job in the Marine Corps. Fortunately for me, this would be the only time in my tour of duty that I would be called on to do this job. It acted as a great motivator for me to stay out of trouble in the future. A life changing event.

While we were busy burning this stuff, our platoon's second squad came walking past us laughing and joking while obviously hiding something under their shirts. They momentarily stopped and showed us what they were carrying. It was some fresh chicken parts and cooking oil they'd just stolen. They had apparently come in from a patrol and just happened to stroll by a field kitchen where the cooks were frying chicken for the officers' evening meal. Being good grunts, Lance Corporal Cavazos and Doc. Rister picked up a few items from the officers galley to take back to their bunker. We were told to hurry and finish up so we could come over with them and get some chicken. They cleaned out one of their empty ammo canisters and filled it with the oil. Everyone started crowding around the homemade fryer, laughing, talking, and waiting for the feast to begin. Everything was going great until without warning, three enemy rockets came flying into the compound from the North. *Blam, blam, blam!* One of the missiles landed next to the squad that was frying the chicken. Cpl. Ron Waugh was killed instantly, and eight others were wounded. Corpsmen came running from everywhere to help the injured that were lying all around. Our outhouse working party was only a hundred yards from the rocket impact and saw everything. This would be my first experience with death to one of the good guys, and it hit me really hard. The trouble with trouble is that it always starts out as fun.

Waugh had just received pictures from his wife of their first child born only a couple weeks before. He was showing his squad the pictures when the rocket landed next to them. The scene had suddenly gone from a big laugh to a big catastrophe in a matter of seconds. Seeing Waugh dead and all the others wounded made it become clearer to me of the deadly seriousness of this place. We had felt like this compound was a secure place where we could be a little more at ease, but it wasn't. Later that day, we were informed that Pfc. Michael Burns had also died from his injuries sustained in the rocket attack.

Through Waugh's and Burns's unexpected death, a lot of emotions came flooding back to me in a personal way about the untimely death of my mom in 1960 and how it had devastated our family. Kilo Company was now my family too, and we had just lost two of our brothers with many more wounded. The pain and sense of loss I was feeling was real as it occurred to me that it hurt no less when these guys died than it did in my own family. This was invariably the kind of emotional trauma I'd always struggle with, helping to create my own never-ending war.

Everyone was told to "get back to your bunkers" in case of another rocket attack or a follow-up assault on our lines. As I got back to my shelter, it was becoming more difficult to shake the sadness and shock about our second squad, coupled with the unhappy memories of our family after my mom's death. Sitting back on the sandbag seat and looking out of the gun aperture, my thoughts were on our family. I decided to write Dad and Paul a short letter while they were on my mind and it was quiet in the compound. I'd forgotten how much I missed my brothers and sisters and wondered if they ever thought about me.

Everyone liked Waugh and Burns, and their deaths had stunned the whole platoon. We had made the mistake of thinking that C-2 base was a relatively safe place, forgetting that being in a fixed compound was like fishing in a barrel. We made an easy target by being so tightly compacted together into one place. Being out in the wide open bush didn't seem so bad anymore, and we could hardly wait to get back out where we could move undetected again. Around sunset the same day, we had three more rockets come blazing into the compound. *Blam, blam, blam!* They all landed on the roadway going through the base, causing very little damage except to our morale. The one that had landed next to our second squad just happened to hit in the right spot. The NVA would set up a primitive, handmade launching platform, aim the rocket by guessing the distance to the target, set the firing timer for thirty minutes, and walk away. It was amazing how accurate they had become over time getting their missiles into the compound. Fortunately for us, they rarely hit anything of importance.

Needless to say, after that incident, we stayed close to a bunker or trench when we moved about the compound, trying to not get caught in the open again.

Around noon the next day, a marine troop carrier came roaring down the road at a high speed and crashed through the south gate of the compound. It finally stopped a couple hundred yards inside the base, and the men nearby ran up to the vehicle to see why he was driving so recklessly. They found the driver had been shot numerous times, along with several dead marines in the back of the truck. They had been ambushed on their way out to join up with our Company at C-2. The BNGs, brand-new grunts as they were called, had just arrived in country a couple days before and had not even made it out to the bush yet. Lt. Oliver North's second platoon jumped onto several battle tanks stationed at the base and went out, looking for the enemy ambush team. They returned back to the compound just before dark after finding no one in the area. The NVA had melted back into the jungle to fight another day. The tremendous frustration we were feeling about losing Waugh and Burns would inadvertently cause us to be even more aggressive in finding and killing our adversary in the coming days. We talked about how we would look forward to hunting them down.

On our last night at C-2, I was told to go out on a three-man listening post (LP). We sat up our LP in a ditch that ran along side the road about two hundred yards outside the south gate. We were to be the eyes and ears of the company throughout the night. If we detected enemy movement, we would radio our platoon so they could take immediate defensive actions. Our LP would then have to make it back into the gate without getting shot ourselves by the assaulting troops behind us or the defending marines at our front. Neither option seemed real promising to us.

Our LP position had rolled razor wire running parallel with the ditch we were set up in, along with thousands of land mines planted in the fields surrounding us. We felt pretty safe even though we didn't know for sure if the mines were really there or not. All we could do was hope so. Around midnight, Pfcs Ritchey and Renfro woke me up and said they had movement down the road from us. We listened carefully and could hear someone walking slowly up the road toward us. As we got ready to open fire on them, the moon suddenly came from behind the clouds and revealed a huge wild hog that must have weighed a couple hundred pounds. He was standing in the road about twenty feet from us, and his white tusks were shining in the moon light.

Renfro whispered, "Should we shoot him?" Ritchey and I snickered and concurred that we might only make him mad. He must have heard us talking because suddenly, he bolted to his right and jumped the ditch, plowing through the barbed wire and into the mine field. After only running a few yards—*wham!*—a mine blew him to smithereens.

Yes! We were now positive there were mines planted around the base. We reported to Lieutenant Haskell about the hog and what had taken place. He then ordered us to suspend our listening post and come back into the compound. He also wanted to know if we could retrieve any part of the dead pig for barbecuing. Grabbing up our gear, we walked back to our bunker where we spent the remainder of the night on line watch.

The next morning, we moved out of the compound as Lima Company moved in to take our place. We would be out in the bush for two or three weeks, patrolling and pulling ambushes around the area known as Leatherneck Square. It never left our minds or conversations about hoping to run into the gook ambush team that had slaughtered the marines in the truck. We wanted to play a little payback on them as retribution. I didn't realize how everyday things were rapidly changing me mentally. I was becoming more callused and hardened by the day. We actually looked forward to finding the enemy and annihilating them without mercy. The idea of killing them on sight would keep them from killing us later, and that only made sense to us. It was one less NVA soldier I had to worry about in the future. All other reasoning went out the window after you learned that law of the jungle.

Fitting In

I quickly found out that part of fitting in with our squad was taking my turn walking point. It was a very serious assignment to undertake because you were the first man in the column to spot trouble or be spotted by the enemy. Most of the others didn't particularly like walking point, but they didn't trust just anyone with the job either. You had to have a good sense of direction, sight, hearing, and smell to be good at the task. The point man has to overcome his fear of being caught off guard by the enemy, and by the definition of *courage*, you have to become a little braver than your greatest fear. That was not easy, but it was necessary to do the job. During my time in Vietnam, I never stopped being scared, but I never let fear stop me from doing what I had to do. For me, walking point was not a problem. If I wasn't up front in the column, I'd usually take up shadow-man position right behind the point man. That way, it was like having two men taking the front position instead of one. I never felt better or braver than anyone else, I just let my fear work for me. It made me cautious, and I trusted my instincts, so why not take point rather than someone else? No one ever complained about me volunteering too much as they just moved aside and said, "Have at it!" It was years later before I realized that much of the damage done to my nervous system came from walking point so often and subjecting myself to an over abundance of fear.

We continued patrolling outside of C-2 base for a week without having any major firefights. We did, however, encounter small groups of NVA which made every minute in the bush seem like walking a tightrope. At any moment, your life could end or be radically changed forever. Not only did we have the enemy to find before he found us, we had the heat and environment to deal with also. It would get upward of 120 degrees that brought on heat casualties. Our rear battalion area would send water to us in six-gallon artillery canisters that had been washed out with a strong detergent and not rinsed very well. The water tasted horrible, so we would fill our canteens with water from bomb craters or ditches. We were given iodine tablets to purify the water, which made it taste even worse. The only way to drink it was to hold our breath and swallow. Otherwise, it would turn our stomach. I asked my dad to send some presweetened Kool-Aid to put in my canteens to help make the water taste better. Dad thought the presweetened cost too much, so he always sent me the unsweetened kind. I knew he loved me, but he just didn't understand that I didn't have any sugar to sweeten it with. He, like most Americans, had no idea what living in the bush was like.

Simply eating and drinking in the wilds was unlike anything I've ever experienced in my lifetime. The adjectives like *dirty*, *stinking*, and *nasty* seemed to leave our vocabulary as we tended to make do with what we had. We figured that if you haven't been thirsty enough to drink water out of a feces-laden rice paddy, you haven't really been thirsty. Believe me, doing so was not by choice.

An Experienced Leader

Our platoon commander, Second Lt. Bill Haskell had been in Vietnam longer than the other field officers of Kilo Company and had a reputation for being very knowledgeable in the bush. We thought he was a little too petty about some things, but sloppiness in the field was no option. A lack of discipline could cost men their lives, and he would try to make sure we would have the best chance to survive Vietnam. He would soon be tested in the harshest of ways and found to be a good leader of marines in March of 1969.

Battle For Mai Loc

During the past two weeks, Kilo Company had been running search-and-destroy patrols from C-2 to the marine artillery base ten miles south called the Rock Pile, named for obvious reasons. Both of these bases were highly beneficial to 3/3 as elements of artillery support in the infamous meat-grinder area. The grunts had to patrol around these critical locations constantly to keep the NVA from building up their forces to attack these bases. Up to this time in the patrol, we had only encountered hit-and-run tactics with the NVA, but things were about to change. The small firefights we had been engaging were just helping to hone up our skills for the next major battle to come.

During the first week of March, we walked out of the bush and up onto Route 9 Highway where we were loaded onto trucks heading south, toward a village called Mai Loc. The village had a large ARVN, SVA (South Vietnamese Army) compound based there for security, but it was mainly for show. They wanted our help in finding and destroying a company of NVA regulars that were operating in the area. They were killing the tribal elders and forcing the peasant villagers to feed and care for them while they acted out their terrorist activities in the region. The ARVNS seemed to be outnumbered, outgunned and out motivated in the fight with the NVA forces. The ARVN base at Mai Loc was circular in design with a high fence running through the center of it. The ARVN soldiers manned half of the compound, and the Americans manned the other half. We never had much to do with the SVA because they were all mixed in with undercover NVA soldiers, and we could never tell the good guys from the bad ones. They were also known for trading sides in the middle of a battle and jump onto the side that was winning. I suppose all Civil Wars are like that. We had never been with them in a real fight, and in our opinion, they were not much more than a mob who liked to wear snug-fitting camouflaged uniforms. They looked real pretty, but when it came to fighting, we didn't think there was much to them.

While at Mai Loc, we got a new commanding officer named Captain Paul Goodwin. He was a no-nonsense type of officer that immediately let us know he demanded much from his officers and enlisted men under his command. This was his second tour of duty in Vietnam, and we could tell from the get-go that he was a seasoned officer. The first thing that Captain Goodwin did was make all the officers shave off their mustache. He told them that the time for doing things their way was over and the time for doing things his way was here. He liked to lead by example, and that was what his officers were also going to do.

The captain didn't make a lot of friends at first, but he did make Kilo Company a better fighting unit. We had been without a company commander for a few weeks, and we had gotten a little slack in some areas. It was like "when the cat is away, the mice will play" thing. He started right away to tighten up on any slackness he found within the company. Within a very short time, we were back to being a highly efficient marine rifle company again. It is said that children do not like authority, but they need it to make them feel secure. We were starting to feel real secure with Captain Goodwin at the helm.

Running Patrols

During the time we were at Mai Loc compound, one platoon would go out into the bush for three days to search for the NVA presence in the area. We would try to make contact with them through ambushes at night and patrols during the day. The other two platoons would stay and man the perimeter at the base compound. They would also be on standby in case the platoon that was running patrols would make contact with the NVA and need reinforcements quickly. They could respond and be on site with the embattled platoon in about thirty minutes.

First Platoon under the command of Second Lt. Bill Haskell was the first one to go out for a three-day patrol. We had zero contact but saw a lot of evidence confirming the NVA presence around the village. After three days of searching, we returned back into the compound, and the second platoon went out to run patrols. Once we got back inside the perimeter, we found it was good to be in the compound again because we could relax a little more than we could out in the bush. The difference was that out in the bush, we had to stay hypervigilant all the times, never knowing when things would suddenly change and when we would be thrown into a firefight with the enemy. We knew a full company of NVA troops were still operating in this area, and it was exciting to imagine us finding them and the firefight that would ensue. The danger level stayed high as our platoons continued to play a deadly checker game with the NVA Company. They would move, and we would move until one of us would make a mistake. We just hoped it wouldn't be us making the misstep because someone was going to die before this game ended.

Back in the Compound

On our first day back inside the compound, one of the ARVN soldiers came over to the fence that divided the marines from them and asked if we wanted to buy some rice whiskey. We told him we did, and he took off to a nearby hooch and quickly returned with a fifth of whiskey under his shirt. He put the bottle through the fence and held his other hand out for the money. We gave him the money, and he took off leaving Ritchey, Pickle, Cavasas, Rudisell, and I to take turns drinking the liquor. Because he had paid for the alcohol, Rudisill appropriately took his turn first. He opened the bottle and put it to his lips and started to take a big swallow. As he turned the bottle upside down in the sunlight, the liquor began to shake up in the bottom of the bottle. We watched as it seemed to implode with glass slivers swirling throughout the liquid. We quickly snatched the bottle away and showed him what he was about to drink. It made us all mad at what had just almost happened to one of our guys, and we were ready to rip out the ARVNs heart for what he'd tried to do.

Fortunately, it hadn't worked, and now our sweet revenge was about to take place. We shouted to the soldier to bring us another bottle right away. He heard us and came running back over with the second bottle and pushed it through the fence as he held out his other hand to take the money from us. I wondered if he was surprised by our wanting another bottle of glass-laced liquor. We all smiled as we grabbed both of his hands and took the bottle from him. He struggled to get free, but we held him tight. We then reached through the fence and grabbed his head, holding it back as we poured the first bottle of whiskey down his throat, glass and all. He coughed and choked but, eventually, got it all down. We let him go, and he staggered off into the unknown to probably die from the glass shavings.

It served him right for trying to kill us. Several of his friends came running over to help him out, but the damage was done. We all laughed and told them to bring it on. They backed off and helped carry their friend away. We checked the second bottle and saw that it was okay. We sat down later that afternoon and enjoyed drinking the glass-free whiskey. It reminded us that we couldn't trust anyone outside of Kilo Company.

The Checkered Board

One of the areas our platoon had been patrolling was an abandoned rice paddy that was dried up and had not been flooded with water in years. The rice paddy dikes were all grown up with hedges that were about four feet wide and ten feet high. The rice paddy area covered about a thousand square yards. It resembled a giant checker board from the air, but from the ground, it looked like a ambush haven. When we walked out of one square sur-rounded by hedges, we would be in another one, just like the first. It was a perfect place to pull ambushes, and we knew the gooks would be setting up concealed positions to ambush us, just like we were for them. It was without question the deadliest terrain we would ever have to fight in. It was apparent that somebody was going to eventually have a bad day, or night, in that area, and we hoped it wouldn't be us.

It seemed like in no time at all, it was our turn to go out again. First Platoon would go out again for a three-day search-and-destroy mission, breaking up into three squad-size patrols to cover more ground in the short amount of time we had. On the first day out, around five o'clock in the afternoon, the second squad led by Cpl. B. J. Miller quietly walked up on a group of NVA soldiers hiding in a banana grove. L/Cpl. Wayne "Reb" Williams, a six-foot-two Alabamian that wore a Confederate Army cap along with a huge bowie knife hanging from his side, was walking point and heard the noise of soldiers digging up turnips they had planted earlier. They were quietly talking to each other as we crawled up behind a low rice paddy dike and watched them from about fifty feet away. We could see they had uniforms on, and their AK47 rifles were leaning against the nearby trees. There were a couple of them act-ing as lookouts, but they had not detected the marines crawling up behind them in the bushes.

Our third squad was summoned to the scene by Miller and quickly joined the second squad for the impending ambush that was about to take place. Cpl. Tom Rudisill then contacted Lieutenant Haskell on our squad radio and told him that we had caught a dozen NVA soldiers off guard, and we were getting ready to open fire on them. To our surprise, Haskell told us to stand down and not do anything until he came to where we were. Reluctantly, we stayed quiet until the rest of the platoon arrived and joined up with us. As we impatiently waited to find out what was the holdup, the NVA soldiers began finishing up their task and started getting ready to leave, causing us to lose our chance at ambushing them. We were all bewildered at the delay and started to get really anxious at the thought of losing this rare opportunity.

They were such an easy target at a short range of thirty yards. I took aim on one soldier and then anticipated the next one to shoot. We could have gotten them all with one burst of our rifles, but we were again told by Rudisill to don't shoot. Finally, Lieutenant Haskell crawled up beside us, announcing that we had to wait until six o'clock before we could open fire on anyone. *What?* Lieutenant Haskell was under strict orders to stand down and could be court-martialed if he disobeyed them. There was a curfew in place that said we couldn't shoot anyone in that area between 6:00 a.m. and 6:00 p.m. because of the civilians working around Mai Loc. The problem was that these people were not civilians. They had uniforms on and were heavily armed. This was the enemy that we had been looking for. Reb flew into a rage as he and Lieutenant Haskell got into a heated argument that almost went to fists being thrown while Rudisill was trying to mediate between the two of them. Even though they were muffling their voices, they started talking so loud the NVA heard them and opened fire on us. We returned fire but had lost our element of surprise.

It turned into a running firefight where no one got hit, or at least, we couldn't find any of them dead or wounded. Lieutenant Haskell told Reb that he was going to be given a court-martial for his insubordination, but I don't think he ever took actions against him because of the awkwardness of the situation. We were all upset because we knew we had lost a good opportunity to waste a squad of NVA that we would now have to find and fight later. Everyone was unnerved for one reason or another. My question was, When did we start fighting a war that had fighting hours?

A Short Time Later

We pulled back to the hedge rows, and Lieutenant Haskell sent out our three squads in different directions. Each squad would set up their own ambush several hundred yards apart. With a full company of NVA roaming around the vicinity, we stood a good chance of making contact in at least one of the ambush sites, if not all three. It was a little scarier now because the NVA knew we were here, and they would be looking for us throughout the night. We were just a platoon against a company, and now we're the ones being hunted. Great!

On our second night in the bush, just about sunrise, the whole company of NVA soldiers came walking through the hedge row area. Corporal Miller's second squad was hiding behind one of the hedge rows when they came passing by. Only three or four marines were awake on watch when they realized the NVA were already among them. They began to quietly wake up everyone in the ambush site. The marines knew they had to act quickly but had no way of knowing they were outnumbered twelve to one. As the horde of soldiers filed by the twelve-man ambush, Miller and Rudisill realized the marines were out gunned by a full company of NVA and made the decision to let them pass on by. As fate would have it, one of the passing enemy soldiers had to relieve himself, so he stopped and stepped into the bushes. Standing still at the edge of the hedgerow, he heard a noise on the other side and stuck his head through to investigate. As he did so, both Reb and Macintosh opened fire on the intruder with full automatic on their M16 rifles, and the firefight was on.

The entire ambush opened up with everything they had. M16s, M60 machine guns, M79 grenade launchers, grenades, and claymore mines that had been strategically set out earlier in the evening to catch as many aggressors as possible in their deadly spray of shotgun pellets. The NVA Company was ripped apart. It was like kicking over an ant hill as they spread out in all directions, taking cover throughout the hedge rows all around them. Second squad's radioman, Lance Corporal Pickle, began to shout on the squad radio, "Contact, contact! We need help right away." Lieutenant Haskell told his other two squads to hurry up and rally on second squad's position. We would then reorganize our platoon as we continued our assault on the NVA Company. Fortunately for us, the NVA didn't know there were so few marines or they would have immediately turned and overrun the twelve-man ambush team. Instead, they scattered. Thank the Lord! My dad must have been praying for me again.

After realizing that we were outnumbered and the NVA had scattered everywhere, Lieutenant Haskell positioned us on one line, side by side, a few yards apart. We opened fire on the hedge-row directly in front of us while the lieutenant called Captain Goodwin for reinforcements. We would begin a search-and-destroy operation to flush out all the hiding enemy soldiers before they could get away or counterattack us. Whatever we were going to do, we couldn't wait for the added support to show up. Haskell had us to stand up and started moving forward through the first hedgerow, firing on anything that looked like a human figure in the bushes in front of us. We pressed on through the second and then the third and so on until we reached the last hedgerow.

Thanks to the leadership of Lieutenant Haskell, we killed about twenty five NVA soldiers and took two prisoners. We also knew that there were always more enemy casualties who had been carried off the battlefield, so we wouldn't find them. In all the fighting we had gone through that day, we only sustained one wounded marine. The results were amazing. A half hour or so into the fighting, Captain Goodwin and Lt. Ollie North's second platoon showed up riding on about six huge M48 battle tanks that were stationed at Mai Loc. Talk about the Calvary showing up. It was a magnificent sight to behold. We knew at that moment, the battle was on our side, and it really felt good.

This had been the biggest and fiercest firefight I'd been in so far. As we moved forward, I spotted a man's silhouette in the hedgerow about twenty yards ahead of me and opened fire. I fired a whole magazine of eighteen bullets at him. I knew it seemed like an overkill, but I was scared and just wanted to make sure he didn't shoot me. I started to go into the bushes and pull him out, but Corporal Rios called for us to continue moving forward, so I left him where he laid. A few minutes later, L/Cpl. Gary Kobra hollered for me to look back toward the one I'd shot. Second platoon was following up behind us, pulling out the dead enemy soldiers from the bushes, collecting their weapons and gear, and dragging them to a collection point near a bomb crater. I felt strangely proud as my buddies were congratulating me on getting my first confirmed kill. It was what we were there to do, and that simply meant that this one would never hurt any of our men again. We kept moving forward until we were sure we had gotten all of them that had stayed back to fight us.

After finishing up our sweep of the area, we pulled back to where we had two POWs and a whole lot of mutilated bodies. I had never seen anything like the carnage I was now looking at. One unfortunate soldier jumped underneath a tank in hopes of blowing it up. Big mistake! The tankers realized that he was under them and began to spin the tank in a circle until it spit the dead, mutilated body out. He was just a heap of twisted, torn-up flesh and bones. He'd been eaten alive by a meat grinder. I learned a valuable lesson from him: never jump under a battle tank to try and blow it up.

You can't crawl faster than what that thing can spin. Another enemy soldier had an M79 grenade round blow up at his feet. It blew his legs apart and ripped him open from his groin to his throat, spewing out all his internal organs. He was lying on his back with all his insides lying seemingly intact on top of him. One of the corpsmen came over to where I was standing and said, "Look at this." He knelt down and took a stick and gave me an anatomy class, showing me all the guy's organs. There was another one that had been shot in the forehead, and his brain had popped out the back of his skull. It was lying beside him, seemingly untouched. Ritchey came over to where I was standing and looked too. He turned to walk away and slipped on something in the grass. We looked down, and he had stepped on the guy's brain. The sole of his jungle boot was covered in brain matter. Ritchey started cursing and trying to dig the grey matter off of his boot. We both laughed at his dilemma, but it seemed funnier to me than it was to him because he had to clean up his boot before it started stinking.

Lance Corporals Bushey and Salles walked up on one soldier sitting in the hedges with his AK47 lying across his lap. The marines hollered out, "*Chu hoi!*," which, we were told, was Vietnamese for "Give up." Apparently, something was lost in the translation because the enemy soldier thought the marines were surrendering. He started to lift up his rifle, pointing it toward the marines. Salles and Bushey immediately cut him down with their M16 rifles. The jarheads then looked at each other, wondering what *chu hoi* really meant. Oh, well.

Mental Hardness

I finally located the one that I'd killed. He was hit six or eight times in his face causing the high-powered bullets to shatter his skull and his facial bones. It looked like he had been hit in the face with a big frying pan. His head was completely round and flattened out, making him look really weird. I couldn't feel anything remorseful or sorry about killing this guy because I knew he was trying to kill me. Lance Corporal Renfro came over and asked me if he was the one I had killed. I said yeah. We both started looking in his uniform pockets and found out he was an officer. He had a military medal in his shirt pocket that had a picture of an NVA soldier shooting at an American helicopter. He must have been a platoon commander or higher to have received it for his unit shooting down a helicopter. I put the medal in my pocket and then took out his wallet and found a picture of his wife and children. It suddenly dawned on me that he was a real human being with a family, instead of just a target.

We were conditioned to avoid getting too emotional about killing the enemy because it might cause us to hesitate the next time, and he would be the one going through my pockets instead of me going through his. The pictures made me feel a little, unnerved, so I put the wallet back in his pocket along with the medal. I'd learned in Sunday school about the evils of killing people. Now, I knew why. This was war, and it was justifiable homicide, but the way we killed some was immoral. I don't think God ever created us to desecrate each other like this. I knew I'd never view life and death in the same way after that day. I didn't keep any souvenirs that I could have taken off the dead combatants. I don't think it was my being superstitious as much as it was that I had enough gear to carry around without hauling their junk too. I'm not really sure why I didn't. Later in life, I'd regret not keeping the guy's medal. It would have been nice to have as it was the only one I've ever seen, and it was a rare item. It was hard to believe that in only a few weeks, I had become a different person. The savagery of warfare has a way of changing people quickly. The marines in our company were eighteen-, nineteen-, and twenty-year-old young American men. They had been the average apple pie eating, Chevrolet-driving boys who were totally unlike anything we had become in this deadly world we were now living in. There was a total disconnect to humanity as we were forced by survival to block out guilt or compunction in killing our enemy. If he died, I could live.

Becoming Callus Was Not an Option

One of the reasons most combatants were shot more than one time was not because we were mean-spirited and hateful. We always had to be overcautious when walking up to a seemingly dead or mortally wounded soldier. We were told that if they were severely wounded, they would take a grenade and hold it underneath them. When you tried to turn him over, he would grab hold of you, pull the string on the grenade, and blow both of you up. All of us agreed that we were not going to take any chances of being shot in the back by a soldier playing possum. Cruel, maybe so, but you would have had to been there to understand. Besides, they didn't take prisoners. Everyone on both sides of the war wanted to go back home in one piece, and we would do whatever we had to do to get back. I just didn't realize that through my survivor-imposed mentality, I was helping to create my own never-ending war.

I had been taught all my life to be a decent man like my father after he had become a Christian. My dad always helped everyone who needed it. He even made lemonade for the neighborhood kids on hot Saturday afternoons. He was a good man that taught me by example. I thought I'd done pretty good so far or at least until coming to Vietnam. I still went out of my way to help everyone around me, but when it came to fighting the enemy, there were no feelings of mercy at all. I'd carry this attitude throughout my tour in Vietnam, but it would come back to haunt me sometime later in life as I would have to begin to face up to my memories and regrets of 1969.

Once we returned to the compound at Mai Loc, we would be there a few more days while one of the other platoons went out looking for any remnants of the NVA Company we had ambushed. We'd never really know how many we'd killed or wounded because we could not find them. We knew they had a lot more casualties because of the heavy fighting that took place that day. It would go down in the record book as one of the largest ambushes by a squad of marines during the Vietnam War. Lieutenant Haskell had proven his skills as a combat leader of marines and had gained the respect from his superiors and his platoon members alike. He would always be our lieutenant of Kilo Company, First Platoon, 1969. I'd write Dad and tell him about the battle and how I'd gotten the one that hurt my brother Bob. I would have liked to have thought so. I'd also ask him to keep praying for our safety, and PS: Send presweetened Kool-Aid.

Victims of War

March 10, 1969
08:00

After spending a quiet night in the relatively secure compound at Mai Loc, the morning sun rose to find first and third platoons manning the perimeter lines with zero percent contact with the enemy. The calendar was one day closer to my rotation date of returning home, and that was what we all lived for. If I could just dodge the bullet for another eleven months, it would be over for me. At least, that was the way it was supposed to work.

Our work here at Mai Loc was finished, and in a couple of days, we would be heading back out into the bush to look for more enemy combatants. Once we found them, we could continue our quest of defeating them in their own country. Although America had the superior military by far, the deck seemed to be stacked against us because the enemy knew his terrain better than we did. They had been continually fighting for the past fifty years and were familiar with every inch of ground. We were still in the process of learning.

Lieutenant North's second platoon was scheduled to come back in from their three days of patrolling the hedgerow area. They had been looking for survivors from the NVA Company we had slaughtered earlier in the week. Kilo Company would soon be jumping onto a convoy of troop carriers and head back up north to the Rockpile Artillery Base. From that point on, only battalion headquarters knew where we would be going.

Around 08:00, Corporal Rios came over to our fighting hole and informed us that we were to go up to the south gate and meet a water tanker. They were making a routine water run to the other side of the province and needed us to go with them. Pfc. Terry Ruggie, Gary Kobra, and I would act as security for the truck in case they got ambushed along the way. It sounded like a pretty good detail to us. At least, it beat filling sandbags all day.

As we boarded the truck and headed through the village of Mai Loc, the truck engine began making a coughing sound. It sputtered and then suddenly quit running, bringing us to a gradual halt. The driver checked the engine and then informed us that he was going to catch a ride back to Motor Transport. He would then get a mechanic to come back with him to get the truck running again. The assistant driver and the three of us would stay with the truck until they returned. We each found a soft place on the truck to lean back and tried to take full advantage of the down time we were getting.

As we were sitting around the vehicle talking, a bunch of kids came up and surrounded us begging cigarettes, candy and C rations. We really didn't have anything to give them except cigarettes, and these kids were only seven or eight years old, so we just talked. They were just like American kids that rattled off questions to us about everything. We talked, laughed, and kidded around with them until their grandmother came out of a hut and called for them to come home. I asked them where they were going, and one of them said, "To eat!" I replied back to them, "Hey, man, take us with you." They instantly grabbed our hands and started pulling on us to go with them. They were saying, "Come on, Marine. We feed you. Come on."

Forgetting about the danger lurking behind every corner, the idea of a home-cooked meal won out over good common sense. We left the assistant driver with the truck and took off with the kids. The driver told us we were crazy for going, and he did not trust them, but we continued on anyway. We held our weapons ready for any signs of trouble, and we reminded each other to stay alert as we made our way to where the woman was standing by the hut door. From the truck, we could see that the kids were gathering at a window on the side of a house. The large opening on the side had a bar that divided the inside from the outside, and the kids were standing at the bar, waiting to eat.

An elderly grandmother inside was stirring something in a kettle that was simmering over an open fire on a dirt floor. She was cooking a mixture of small fish and vegetables in some kind of tomato sauce that smelled really good to us. There was also an elderly man with her that was sitting on a bench next to where she was cooking. He looked harmless enough as he appeared to be a village elder with his long, thin beard hanging down and dressed in their customary silk pajamas. They were both acting giddy as he passed her plates to serve the strange-looking visitors their grandchildren had brought home unannounced. The lady dished out the concoction onto several different kinds of plates and passed them to everyone. Behind her, on the wall was a shelf that had about a dozen four-inch high glasses on it. In each glass was about an inch of dark liquid. She took down one glass at a time and shook it out onto the dirt floor. She then filled each one with fresh tea that tasted like sassafras and passed it on to each of us. As we took the glasses from her, we sniffed the contents and looked at each other. We thanked her and toasted the event by saying, "Whatever."

We all smiled at the sweet couple that was offering their best to a bunch of dirty, sweaty marines. Everything happening around us seemed to be the normal way with this family, so we just continued to go along with the program. We had been told at Camp Pendleton, California, to always be polite to the civilians in Vietnam. They told us to always leave a little food on your plate and a little drink in your glass as a sign to your host that you were satisfied and had more than you could eat or drink. If you didn't, they could be embarrassed and insulted if they didn't have anymore to serve you. The food was really spicy, but it tasted good. I left a little on my plate and rubbed my stomach to let them know how much I'd enjoyed her cooking. The tea looked strong, and the glasses appeared to have never been washed, so I held my breath and downed the entire contents of the glass. *Oops!* I forgot to leave a little bit of the tea. The lady promptly refilled my glass with more liquid and gave me a big smile, showing her solid black teeth that were created from chewing the beetle nut, a drug that turned their teeth as black as coal over time. She seemed really proud of them.

I drank the next glass of tea, leaving about an inch of the substance in it. She cleared the bar of all the dishes and took everyone's glass and put them back on the little shelf until next time. Because of the language barrier, we used body language to make sure the couple knew how much we appreciated their hospitality. The kids had brought our lives together with a little food, and we had gotten to meet some very nice people for a change. We just hoped their kindness would not cause them any trouble from their neighbors because we had seen several people looking at us eating with this family. The NVA would have killed the whole family if they thought they were fraternizing with us.

We thanked them and returned to the truck where the hungry and disgruntled truck driver was patiently waiting. He told us how scared he was, standing by the truck all by himself. We laughed and told him, "Get over it!"

The driver and mechanic had recently returned, and the truck was ready to go. We loaded up and took off down the road. It had been a nice experience for the three of us, and we ended up having a pretty good day for a change. It was the only time I would get a chance to eat with a Vietnamese family, and I was glad we did. It also helped me to realize that I was not completely bad, and I still had feelings for good and innocent people everywhere.

Grunts spent a lot of time out in the bush, and we never ran into good people out there, only the ones that were trying to kill us. It gave us a slanted view of the Vietnamese people.

The Road Sweep

March 11, 1969

The next morning, we had to run a patrol between two villages that were about ten miles apart with a bridge along the way, crossing over a small stream. The civilians would carry their goods from one village to the other in hopes of selling their merchandise. They used a long pole on their shoulder and suspended a basket on each end. Each basket would be loaded with as much stuff as the person could balance and carry. It amazed us to how much weight they could bear in those baskets. We arrived at the bridge some time later and checked it for demolitions that the NVA might have set the night before. The bridge was clear, so we stood at both ends of it and checked the baskets the women were carrying for contraband like drugs or weapons. The ladies would put their baskets on the ground and step back letting us check them without complaint. They would then pick up their stick with the baskets hanging on each end and begin walking down the steep incline, continuing on their journey. We told them that it was safe to cross the bridge, but they didn't believe us. They would take the long way around even though it was much harder and longer because they simply thought it was safer.

Along with the older women in one group was a pretty young girl in her midteens that ended up stopping next to me. Her baskets were filled with of bottles of wine that probably weighed as much as she did. The thought came to me about helping this pretty girl up the steep incline with her heavy burden. I nodded my intentions to her and politely took the stick and placed it on my shoulder, picking up the two baskets. I was shocked because they must have weighed eighty pounds or more. As I strained and groaned beneath the load, all the older ladies started laughing as they watched me laboring under the weight of the young girl's load. My pride would not let me put the baskets down, so I carried them down the hill, across the stream, and up the far side of the hill. I was exhausted by the time I reached the road again. It was then that the thought struck me: Why didn't I just walk across the bridge?

Duh! I put the thing down, and she took the contraption from me and nodded a thank you as they all took off waddling away at a fast-walking pace. The older ladies were still laughing and mocking me as they moved on down the road. My buddies were also laughing at my stupidity of hitting on the young girl.

I mused over the thought of how American women had it so easy back home. Maybe they should come over here and see how these women live. Perhaps they would be a little more appreciative of their easy lifestyle.

As we began the second half of our road sweep to the village, we started seeing blood spots on the dirt road we were walking on. We went on high alert as we started stalking the apparently wounded person. We soon came around a curve and spotted the elusive culprit—an elderly woman walking along the road, spitting red beetle nut juice. We all chuckled and agreed it was good that it had turned out to be nothing. The roadway we were traveling on had been cut through a mountain with high cliffs on both sides. At one point in the road, we looked up and saw about twenty mountain people, Montagnards, standing on the edge of the cliffs and looking down on us. They looked extremely menacing because they were all holding highly functional crossbows along with sickles and big knives. They looked like Aborigines from Australia because they practiced intermarriage within their families. Some of them actually were deformed, and their faces were disfigured.

As I gazed at them, a thought came to me: please don't shoot me with an arrow. It looked like a very painful and a cruel way to die. The mountain people generally stayed to themselves and had very little to do with anyone outside of their culture. We might run into one of their villages out in the jungle but very seldom saw them out in the open. We were glad they were on our side of the war because they were courageous fighters with their primitive but effective weapons. They were considered outsiders by the Vietnamese people mainly because they lived in the bush and had their own counterculture. They were definitely on the bottom of the Vietnamese cultural totem pole. All we cared about was that they were our allies, and they could be trusted. We could depend on them, and we had one thing in common—they considered the NVA their enemies. And that made the enemy of our enemy our friend. We waved at them and kept walking until we got passed them and then breathed a sigh of relief.

A Violent People

On one occasion when we were at C-2 artillery base, an NVA soldier went into a village outside the base and killed a Montagnard elder who was trying to apprehend him. The mountain people caught the soldier as he was trying to escape. They tied him to a pole in the center of the village and skinned him alive. They told the marines to mind their own business, and we did. That was their kind of justice system.

Leaving Mai Loc

The next day, we left Mai Loc and went back up to the Rock Pile Artillery Base. We used the base many times to resupply between and during operations in the meat grinder, and this time would be no different. I wrote my dad and told him about eating with the Vietnamese family and reminded him to keep praying for us. We needed God's help to get us through this mess. PS: Send food especially presweetened Kool-Aid.

Operation Virginia Ridge

On May 2, 1969, Third Battalion, Third Marines began an action called Operation Virginia Ridge. Kilo Company had pulled out of Con Thien combat base for the DMZ and surrounding areas. They had been at the base just long enough to receive replacements and refit worn out equipment. Along with the new marines joining Kilo, the company was still only 185 men strong and heading into the most dangerous area of Vietnam. With several operational goals to meet along the way, it would take around eighteen grueling days to get up to Mutter's Ridge by foot.

During the eighteen days of patrolling, the company had started out by jumping on a heavily armored convoy and trucked to the Rock Pile Artillery Base. There, we were put back again on our most reliable form of transportation—our feet. Since then, Kilo Company had been walking and fighting its way north toward the ominous ridgeline that towered above them. Kilo Company arrived at the base of the ridgeline on May 20 and continued operations around the grasslands, in eight-to-ten-foot high elephant grass, for the next four days. The thick grass itself was wicked to walk through because we couldn't see more than two feet in front of us. On one afternoon patrol, I was shadow man for Private First Class Grogan and helplessly watched him walk right off a cliff. He was fortunate to only fall about twenty feet down where he landed on some thick grass, avoiding injury. He looked back up to me, and we both fell out laughing at his sudden dilemma. The thin blades of grass were sharp and would cut exposed sweaty skin, causing an infection which scabbed over constantly running with pus. It generally grew into what the marines termed jungle rot that grew larger wounds if not treated twice each day until it healed.

Pfc. Donald Liebl had the misfortune of sitting down on a stick that rose up out of the ground a couple of inches. It scratched the inside of his rectum. Twice every day, he went to Doc Hrzic and dropped his trousers. He would then bend over and let Doc. scratch the wound until it bled. Doc would then splash a good amount of iodine onto the wound, and Donald would go running off, trying to cool down his injury. It was comical to watch, but at the same time, we pitied Liebl. During his ordeal, they became close friends. Liebl admired Doc Hrzic and asked him why he was there. He was smart and was going to become a doctor after he returned home. Liebl would then say that he was dumb and had nothing going for him. He deserved to be there, and this was where he was supposed to be. Doc Hrzic was wounded in August, and he returned home. Liebl was killed in September.

As Operation Virginia Ridge continued, the other three companies in the battalion were moving into place around the ridgeline to act as a search-and-destroy operation but also to be able to respond to Kilo Company if they needed support in their mission to go into the DMZ.

By morning of May 24, the company had lost quite a few marines from being wounded in firefights and deathly sick with malaria. We were down to four of the seven officers and 159 men. We had lost twenty-six men so far, and we hadn't even gotten into the DMZ yet.

Early that morning, the first platoon was sent out on a short patrol to make sure the NVA wasn't following or trying to move in on us. This was their territory, and they were amassing all around us as we were preparing to assault the ridgeline and Hill 410 the next morning. As we patrolled through the high grass, I started to feel nauseous and feverish. I first thought it was the heat and high humidity because it was sweltering hot. By the time we got back to the company area, I was not feeling good at all. I found Doc Hall and asked him to check my temperature. He took it and said it was 101 degrees. He told me to sit in the shade and to not smoke any more cigarettes until he took my temperature again later on. A couple of hours later, it was 102 degrees and climbing. I went back to the shade again and lay down. I was feeling terrible.

Doc Hall called for me just before dark and said that our company commander, Capt. Paul Goodwin, told him that there was only one more chopper coming in and if my temperature wasn't 103 degrees or higher, I wasn't going anywhere. He took my temperature as the last chopper was coming in and saw it was 103 degrees. He tagged me for medevac, and I ran back to my squad and quickly distributed my gear among them. I told them to take care, and along with two other sick marines, we jumped on the chopper.

We soon found out that before the medevac chopper came after us, they had first stopped at Lima Company's position. Lima was engaged in a heavy battle somewhere down on the ridgeline, and the chopper had picked up some of their dead and wounded. The helicopter was full of blood, and there were several bodies wrapped in ponchos to keep the flies and bugs off them. The carnage inside the chopper was terrible.

Forty-five minutes later, we landed at a MASH unit field hospital in Con Thien where I was stripped down and given a cold shower to try and get the fever down. My temperature had risen to 105-plus degrees, and I was beginning to feel delirious and uncoordinated. If I had missed getting on that last chopper coming in, I probably would have died during the night due to my high fever. There were a lot of marines and army soldiers coming into the hospital with malaria. A group of us were taken to third medical hospital where I was led into a ward and put in a bed between two refrigerated pads. In a matter of minutes, those painfully cold blankets broke my fever and started bringing my temperature down to a more controlled level. At the foot of my bed was a young marine lying in a bathtub full of ice. A corpsman nearby told me the guy's temperature was 107 plus. He added that if he survived through the night, he would be a vegetable. I thought, *He came over here to fight and a mosquito took him out.* I felt sorry for him and his family.

Within a few hours, my temperature finally settled close to the normal range, and they choppered me and several others out to the *USS Sanctuary* hospital ship that traveled several miles off shore, up and down the coast of Vietnam. No doubt that this ship had saved many lives as it traveled the coastline. As our chopper landed, we were taken below deck and led to a ward for malaria patients. A corpsman took me to the head (bathroom) where they had showers with seats in them. It had been a long time since I had been in a hot shower. The corpsman stayed with me in case I passed out while taking this wonderful bath. Afterward, he gave me some pajamas and escorted me to a top bunk. The doc pulled back the starched sheets and helped me climb in. He tucked me in, and I slept for twenty-four hours before waking up again. Malaria was an unbelievably wonderful experience.

While I was sleeping, they pumped me full of quinine to kill the malaria, but it didn't bother me at all. It was the best sleep I'd had in a long time. I woke up a day later to see a television playing across the room along with a cold-water fountain next to my bunk. It took me a minute or so to adjust to having these luxuries again while lying in my soft bed. It had only been four months since I'd lost all these comforts, but it seemed a lot longer. While lying in my comfort zone, my thoughts turned to my buddies up on Mutter's Ridge. I wondered what they were doing and how bad it had gotten up there. I couldn't help from missing them a little and felt a strange feeling of guilt for not being with them in such a dangerous place. Oh, well, there was nothing to do for the time being but lean back and enjoy my small vacation of soft beds, hot food, cold drinks, hot showers, and pretty nurses. As weird as it sounds, malaria was one of the best things that happened to me in Vietnam.

After a week of quinine shots and rest, I was flown to a hospital in Da Nang for another three days of observation. On my last day there, I was assigned to a flight back to our battalion rear area at Quang Tri for three days of light duty before going back into the bush. I had heard that Kilo Company had been ambushed five days in a row, and every time they were ambushed, the NVA would wound or kill from three to five of our men. I knew they desperately needed experienced reinforcements. I found out that just a couple days before, the company had been in the largest firefight of the operation in June 11. They had assaulted and had taken a bunker complex where they had lost four marines along with several wounded. Three helicopters were hit coming in for the wounded, and the company had to go to an alternative LZ (landing zone) where it was safer to land the choppers. My high fever must have warped my brain because I wanted to get back out there with them, and I figured they could use the extra help.

I requested permission to return to the company in spite of my light-duty status and was granted authorization. A short time later, I jumped onto a chopper along with a bunch of BNGs and took off for the bush. As our chopper approached Kilo Company's position on Hill 410, we could see that they were under a mortar attack. Two or three Huey gun ships were firing their weapons at an adjacent hill, trying to destroy an NVA mortar team that was dropping their deadly barrage on Kilo Company's position. In a few minutes, the enemy mortars would be silenced, and our chopper would be landing on a hot LZ, putting me back into the war again. About that time, the thought hit me: I still had three days of light-duty rest in the rear area. What am I thinking?

Back in the War Again

The Final Days of Virginia Ridge

During the time I was out with malaria, Kilo Company continued conducting Operation Virginia Ridge in and around the DMZ area. The story of what took place during that time was later featured in a Leatherneck magazine article in July 2000, "Firefight on Mutter Ridge." It was written by our commanding officer, then Capt. Paul Goodwin, Kilo 6. With only a few change of names and personal additions to the narrative by other First Platoon Marines, the story is consistent with Captain Goodwin's account. All the men of Kilo Company will forever be grateful to Colonel Goodwin for sharing our story with the world about our going into the DMZ to capture an NVA prisoner. It was a daring operation that we were able to pull off largely due to the superb leadership of the officers of Kilo Company.

This is their story. On the same day I had been medevaced out for malaria, Captain Goodwin was also choppered out of the bush to participate in a command group meeting with all the commanders in third battalion. Major R. Deforest, the battalion's operations officer, issued a five-paragraph order, tasking Kilo Company with moving up on top of Hill 410 and digging in. They would then move eight hundred meters south of the DMZ and establish a patrol base from which they would launch two thirteen-man patrols into the DMZ to capture a prisoner for interrogation. The order stated that there were an estimated two NVA regiments in and around the DMZ area with units up to company size in the southern portion where Kilo Company would be operating.

In the previous four months I'd been with Kilo Company, we had only taken two prisoners of war. The NVA did not normally surrender and taking prisoners was not the usual way of doing things in the meat grinder. Captain Goodwin returned to Kilo Company with his new orders. We would be the second company-sized unit to ever go into the DMZ during the Vietnam War.

The Infamous Mutter's Ridge

Everyone was up and about at sunrise on May 25. All the ambushes and listening post had been brought back in, and they were given a few minutes to eat their C ration breakfast and saddle up. The platoon commanders were given their assignments for the day, and the company started to line up in a column by platoons. First in line was Haskell's first platoon, then Goodwin's command post followed by North's second platoon, and finally, O'Neill's third platoon bringing up the rear security and putting out flanks on both sides of the column to fend off any ambushes along the way. In preparation for the move up the hill, Lieutenant Vandaveer, artillery forward observer, called in barrages on Hill 410 and two other nearby hills, hoping to confuse the NVA about our real objective. After ceasing fire, first platoon stepped off leading the company down the finger of the ridge and through the 8 foot high elephant grass.

Although it was yet still early in the day, a combination of humidity and exertion had the marines sweating profusely because the grass was thick and tough to get through. There were times when the point man, L/Cpl. James Grogan would have to turn around backward and throw himself onto the wall of grass in front of him. The shadow man following him would act as the point man in his stead as they worked as a team. It was particularly dangerous for the point man because he couldn't see what he was walking into. The point man slowly made his way down the finger to a stream about a thousand meters from their night position of the previous night. First platoon was familiar with the area because they had ambushed an enemy mortar team here two days earlier. The smell of decaying bodies was overwhelming, and it was obvious that their comrades had not claimed them for burial.

Kilo Company was at the base of the ridgeline, and it looked like they had about a thousand meters to go before getting to the top where they could set up a defensive perimeter for the night. It started off steep for three hundred to four hundred meters but then began to flatten out a little after that. We soon began to enter the canopy of jungle vegetation hovering above the marines that almost blotted out the sun. It seemed strangely quiet in the shaded area, and the marines began to become extra cautious due to a lack of noise. The only sounds being made were the labored breathing of exhausted marines and an occasional curse at the low-hanging limbs and vines that would seem to reach out and grab you as they were aptly called wait-a-minute vines. The blistering morning sun had become so hot you could hear a high-pitched ringing in your ears, as the column continued moving up the side of the ridge. Suddenly—*boom! boom!*—twin explosions along with automatic weapons fire seemingly coming from everywhere. First platoon had unwittingly walked into an ambush. Their radioman, L/Cpl. Gary Kobra began frantically shouting, "Kilo. Kilo. Kilo 1, my actual's down skipper, My actual's down. We're being overrun. We need help!"

Goodwin gave his hand set to radio operator L/Cpl. Perry Hamler and told him to get Lieutenant North up here right away. "Quick!" Goodwin then turned and yelled to the company gunnery sergeant banner to "get prepared to set up a landing zone anywhere you can find a clearing. We've got to get the wounded out of here as soon as we can." Capt. Goodwin moved forward and helped get first platoon up and moving again from where they had been pinned down. Their first squad had been hit hard, and Haskell was critical. North's second platoon began moving up with first platoon and began laying down a heavy field of fire and counterattack. They had to get the medevacs out and destroy the bunkers up ahead. Goodwin told Vandaveer, "Get artillery going, but keep it well up the hill, and work it back." The marine's 81-mm. and 60-mm. mortar teams were quickly getting their rounds on target within minutes of the opening attack.

Goodwin then radioed Deforest and requested a fire support priority and his help getting the medevac helicopters underway. He also requested a resupply of basic ammunition, grenades, 60-mm. mortar rounds as well as water. When second platoon finally got up to where first platoon had been ambushed, they were shocked by the carnage. Several badly wounded marines lay among the shattered vegetation as corpsmen desperately tried to save their lives. Equipment and debris were scattered everywhere, including abandoned weapons from the injured, helmets, packs, and medical supplies along with several NVA soldiers lying in that tell-tale position of death.

Several first platoon marines had taken a position for covering Lieutenant Haskell who had been severely wounded by shrapnel from a Chicom grenade. He lost his right eye and almost his life in the incident. As the assault was grinding down to a halt, casualties were mounting, and something was needed to restore momentum. Goodwin called out for air support. The enlisted I-4 officer called for immediate air support. He declared, "Troops in contact," a universal signal that someone needs help and fast. The word went out, "Everybody, down, air inbound!"

Two marine F-4s checked in dropping bombs and napalm, but it still didn't knock out the gooks' .50 caliber machine gun. As they departed, two navy F-4s showed up with five-hundred-pound bombs. Lieutenant North threw a smoke grenade further up the hill and told the two jets to drop their bombs about 150 meters beyond that. They hit right on target, but the enemy guns continued blasting. The close air support did wonders for morale but still didn't knock out the guns. Every time the marines started to move forward, the machine gun would come back into action, forcing the marines to the ground as the attack hung in the balance. Suddenly, Cpl. E. Titan jumped up with his M60 machine gun. He cradled it in his arm as he started moving forward, firing at the enemy gunner. The first and second platoons followed up with him as they started over running the bunker complex. They moved through twenty-some bunkers destroying each one as they passed by making sure that no NVA were left alive to shoot them in the back. There was evidence that there had been about forty defenders in the bunker complex at the beginning of the ambush. It was now 17:00, some seven hours after the initial contact. It had been a long, hard day, and Kilo Company was beaten up a little. They had sustained fifteen percent casualties and still had not accomplished their mission. The company still had to go further into the DMZ and capture a prisoner, and the NVA were fully alerted and, in all probability, were preparing to hit back.

Though exhausted, the marines would still have to rotate their three-man watches in each fighting hole all night. This was not a place to let your guard down. If you went to sleep, you had a very good chance of not waking back up. We used every trick we knew to stay awake because sleeping on watch was not an option. We used briers to put beneath our chin to keep our head from dropping down from sleepiness. The pointed thorns would stick into our flesh, keeping us awake. Drinking a little water and splashing the precious liquid on our face would also help, but you hated to waste water unless it was absolutely necessary. Life was tough, but we had no choice.

The next morning, Kilo Company got up at sunrise and moved down the north side of Mutter's Ridge, about eight hundred meters and set up a perimeter. The company was told to keep a heat tablet, which was used to heat their C rations, handy in case we were attacked at night. The grunts would light them in the bottom of their fighting holes during the enemy attack, and aircrafts like Puff or Snoopy would be able to see the heat tablets and avoid opening up their deadly spray of bullets on our perimeter. This is the times of life that will make a young man age quickly, and it will also add volumes to your personal never-ending war, PTSD.

From our company position, Goodwin sent out two thirteen-man patrols, one to the northwest and one to the northeast. About an hour and a half after they departed, the marines at the company position heard the familiar sounds of M16 rifle fire echoing from the direction of the patrol led by Lt. Richmond O'Neill. O'Neill came on the radio and reported killing two NVA soldiers. A few minutes later, fire erupted from Lieutenant North's patrol. He radioed that they had killed two more and captured a wounded prisoner. He had also found a cache of food, supplies, and arms.

O'Neill's patrol was ordered back to the company perimeter. A reaction force went out from the company to meet with North's patrol and relieve him of the POW so he could set up another ambush. They met about a thousand meters inside the DMZ.

Captain Goodwin happily reported the find to Lieutenant Colonel Shultz and requested he be allowed to move the entire company down into the zone and set up ambushes. He was denied because only a certain amount of men were allowed inside the DMZ at a time.

The company pulled back south to Hill 410 located on Mutter's Ridge.

Lieutenant North's thirteen-man patrol was allowed to stay and set up an ambush on the complex while the rest of the company returned to Hill 410. Before leaving the complex the next morning, North's patrol destroyed the supply cache with a huge explosion. They knew the enemy would come looking for them as soon as they heard the blast. They double-timed it back to Hill 410 and rejoined the company.

Kilo Company stayed one more night on the hill, being hit by another mortar attack that caused a few more minor casualties. They received orders to rejoin the battalion and conclude Operation Virginia Ridge. The operation had gone down in the record book as a complete success but also added another chapter into our own never-ending war, PTSD.

Night of Death

Around the twenty-fifth of July, Kilo Company moved out from Con Thien with two platoons of M48 battle tanks led by Capt. Mike Wunsch. This was our first time patrolling on tanks in Leatherneck Square, and the change from walking to riding was a good break from having to haul around our heavy packs. The problem was that there is no way to move quietly on a battle tank with its tracks squeaking and clanking along. The grunts liked being able to move quietly through the bush without being seen, but that was impossible to do on these things.

These great behemoths were visible from a couple of miles away because the brush was thick and low in Leatherneck Square, and they stood out like a sore thumb. We knew the NVA were watching us, and they would attack whenever the opportunity showed itself favorable to them, either by day or night.

About daybreak on the second morning in the bush, we heard mortar tubes firing, creating a popping sound in the distance. A minute or so later, we were hit by several incoming enemy mortar rounds. We dropped our packs and were still diving for cover when the projectiles arrived right on top of us. The inbound missiles made a swooshing sound just before they hit the ground, exploding all around us. Fortunately for us, no one was hit by their shrapnel.

As soon as the incoming mortar attack ended, we began scanning the terrain for any sign of the enemy mortar team. Someone saw a trail of smoke from the mortar tubes in the distance and shouted out their find to the tankers. The smoke looked to be at least a mile away, but it didn't seem to be a challenge for Captain Wunsch's marines to hit their mark. It was so cool to watch the big guns go into action. The turret turned in the direction of the smoke, took aim, and fired one shot right on target. They fired several more rounds, and the mortar was silenced forever. The grunts couldn't help but give out a muffled cheer for the tankers and the impressive exhibition of heavy duty fire power.

After the excitement ended, we saddled up and moved out. Late in the afternoon of July 28, Kilo Company and the thirteen tanks were seven kilometers southwest of Con Thien. The tanks had moved to the highest hill in the area to set up for the night, giving the marines better visibility over the terrain around them. This would be our last night in the bush with the tanks, and everyone was becoming a little anxious in knowing we were escorting a real prize the NVA would love to capture or destroy. It was our third night in the bush, and we wondered if the enemy was mounting a large force to try and claim the prize before we returned to Con Thien in the morning. If they were, it would be tonight. It was now getting late in the afternoon, and we'd soon be finding out their plan.

Lt. Oliver North and his second platoon stayed with the tanks as security in case the NVA tried to attack them during the night. They dug their fighting holes between the large armor-plated monsters hoping to make a good defensive perimeter.

Third platoon, led by Lt. Richmond O'Neill, moved out of the company perimeter and headed north to split up into three different squad-sized ambushes. They were hoping to score some kills if any NVA tried to move into the area to attack the tanks. First platoon, led by their new platoon commander, Second Lt. Eric Bowen headed south to split into three separate ambushes also. They had found three dead NVA soldiers that afternoon, and Lieutenant Bowen and the second squad led by Cpl. Bill Bushey were going to set up an ambush on them, hopeful the NVA would come that night to claim them for burial. I had recently become third squad leader and was told to take my men about two hundred meters down the road and set up our ambush on an intersection of some recently used footpaths. First squad, led by

L/Cpl. Edward Cavazos, moved several hundred yards further down the path from us in order to cover as much area as possible. We found a prefect ambush site and set out our claymore directional mines to surprise any enemy troops moving through the ambush kill zone. The traps were set, and all we had to do now was wait. Around 23:00, Lieutenant Bowen called on our radio and told me that they had movement around the three bodies they had set their ambush up near.

The lieutenant and a couple members from second squad threw several grenades at the intruders as they were trying to carry their fallen comrades away. A couple of minutes later, he called again and said they had left his area and were heading straight toward my ambush. I got everyone awake and alert as we got ready to spring the trap on the unsuspecting enemy soldiers heading our way.

It's hard to explain the emotions one goes through in the moments before your ambush opens fire on other human beings. Lying in the darkness, waiting for your enemy to get close enough so you can kill him. The emotional roller coaster of excitability, numbness, and fear of close combat would all become a major factor in my emotional never-ending war. I would replay the events of this night a thousand times in the years to come, reliving the struggle with life and death and trying to keep my squad members alive throughout the next eight hours. Suddenly, through the darkness, we heard someone running down the path toward us. They were talking and laughing as they unknowingly entered into our ambush kill zone. They must have been thinking about how they'd gotten away with stealing the dead bodies from the marines a few minutes earlier. Bad mistake for them!

As they entered the kill zone directly in front of us, we allowed the first ones to get almost all the way through the ambush site before we opened up on them with our claymore mines. Corporal Rudisell and I pressed the handsets to the five directional mines that we had previously set out. *Wham, wham, wham, wham!* The deadly spray of shotgun pellets from the mines instantly turned the enemy's demeanor from laughing to utter chaos. Our squad then opened fire on the figures that we could now see from the explosions going off. The sight of men being caught in a killing spray of bullets was intense. They were screaming and yelling as they tried to escape the overwhelming fire power they had unwittingly walked into. There was nowhere for them to go as they died where they stood. Our machine gun team began spraying the road in front of us with an M60 to make sure they were all dead. After a few minutes of firing our weapons, I told everyone to cease fire.

As the noise of the gun fire subsided and the darkness returned, we could hear several groans coming from the darkness in front of us. I told Torboli to spray down the road again with his M60 to make sure no one was getting away. Without hesitation, I took out a grenade from my flak jacket pocket and pulled the pin. I whispered, "Frag," to alert my men so they would keep their heads down and not get hit by my grenade shrapnel. I threw it in the direction of one of the moans and *blam!* The grenade exploded, killing the NVA soldier but also hit one of my own men surprisingly. Private First Class McDaniels yelled out, "I'm hit!"

What? I could hardly believe it. I had told everyone to get down, but apparently, he hadn't heard me. He was too busy doing his own thing as he had turned away from the ambush area and was on all fours getting something from his pack. The grenade went off hitting him with several pieces of hot metal in his rear end. Doc Jerry Hrzic had McDaniels to pull down his trousers to reveal his wounds. In the darkness, Doc began looking for all the little shrapnel holes in McDaniels's back side by rubbing his bloody, slippery skin until he had found and patched all the holes. McDaniels once muffled, "I'm on fire!" Between garbled laughter, Doc warned the private first class that if he ever told anyone about what he had just done, he would kill him himself.

Everyone in the ambush site, including Doc Hrzic, was quietly laughing while telling each other to shut up or we were going to give our position away. For a brief moment, life was funny, but then we stopped laughing and proceeded with the deadly business at hand.

Rudisell and I discussed the situation and decided what had to be done in order to preserve the lives of our squad of marines.

Because of so much enemy activity in the area that night, we couldn't just pick up and go to a new ambush spot. It was just too dangerous to move around in the darkness. We had to finish up with the ambush we had started. Rudisell, Ritchey, Pickens, and I went out into the darkness to find and make sure the NVA soldiers were all dead. They were. We didn't have to quiet them, but we would have because we wanted to live. I really didn't want to go out in the darkness with my men especially knowing there were possibly wounded and heavily armed soldiers lying out there with nothing to lose by killing us. Then I remembered my dad's words: "Never ask someone to do what you are too scared to do yourself."

Pickens and I teamed up and went in one direction, and Rudisell and Ritchey went in the other. We found eleven bodies in the ambush site along with a couple of blood trails. Lieutenant Bowen radioed in for artillery illumination flares to be fired from C-2 base. The flares helped us to momentarily see but caused a few problems with moving shadows as they floated down on little parachutes. It was like watching one of the first motion pictures as the light and darkness chased each other. It made us be even more cautious as we searched for live, wounded NVA soldiers in the blackness of night. We found and disarmed all the dead enemy soldiers and dragged them into a pile in front of our ambush site. We left eleven dead bodies in a heap with hopes of more NVA coming by and stopping to investigate the scene. We would then be able to pull another ambush, killing more enemy troops.

Getting back into the ambush site, I took a quick inventory and found out we had used a lot of ammo in the first ambush. There was one claymore mine that had not exploded. We fitted it with a new blasting cap and reset it.

A Larger Battle Taking Place

We noticed a lot of explosions and shooting going on in the distance behind us. My radioman informed me that the tanks were under attack by a large number of NVA estimated to be a battalion in size. We looked at each other in stunned amazement and said, "God help them." They were outnumbered by the enemy twenty to one.

From the tracers bullets dotting the night sky and explosions going off in the distance, second platoon marines along with the tanks were in a fight for their lives, and we could do nothing to help them. Ground combat in the darkness has got to be the worst kind of fighting possible. We could only hope and pray that God would keep them safe, and they would hold on and not be overrun. The tanks were a big plus for the marines, but they were also big targets for the NVA to fire their RPGs (rocket-propelled grenades) at. The tanks were what they came to destroy, and they would not be satisfied until they had accomplished their goal.

Lance Corporal Cavasas's first squad reported they had made contact with an unknown number of NVA. They had been the third ambush from first platoon to make contact that night.

The marines had ambushed a small group of NVA soldiers only minutes after we had pulled ours. We figured they were possibly the ones running from our ambush and got caught in his. The first squad marines had killed six NVA soldiers in their opening volley. Their position was closer to the heavy armor than ours, and they could see RPGs slamming into the tanks and machine gun tracers firing wildly into the dark sky. We listened to the whole battle raging on our squad radio. It was mind-boggling for us to listen to what was happening to our second platoon marines.

By the conversations going back and forth between them, we could tell they were fighting hard to repel the NVA troops. The fighting seemed to lessen as the night went on, but the battle would not be over until dawn. Only then could the marines see who they were fighting. There was a lot of deadly activity in the bush that night, and no one was sleeping. We never knew when the enemy would walk up on our position, and we would be instantly thrown into a fight for our lives. We stayed on a one hundred percent watch throughout the long night. In the early hours before dawn, second platoon radioed that the NVA had broken off fighting and were disappearing into the darkness. They were separating into small groups and heading out in different directions. The enemy was on the move, and we didn't know where they would show up. We had earlier hoped for a chance to pull another ambush, but this was different now, and there might be more than what we could handle. I had a dozen men in my squad, and the thought of having to fight a hundred or so by ourselves was sobering to all of us especially considering the fact that we had spent a lot of ammunition on the first ambush.

My thought was that the chance of them passing nearby without finding us was slim. There were eleven dead NVA soldiers piled out in the road along with the lingering smell of blood and gun powder from the blast and carnage of the earlier battle. We bravely laid in the darkness, hoping and praying they would not find us.

I turned toward the rear of our ambush so I could see anyone coming from behind us. The illumination had ended, and it was pitch dark. The only sound I could hear was my own heart beating and my labored breathing. We all knew that at any minute, we could break out into hand-to-hand fighting as the enemy stumbled upon us in the darkness. I positioned our three fire teams in different directions so the gooks could not walk up on us undetected. We were somewhat convinced they would find us and a firefight would ensue. The only consolation I had was that I was not the only one scared. We all were. When people think about combat, they think about bravery, heroics, and tough guys. We didn't think about any of those things. We were scared. Tonight, we would not fight for glory or medals; we'd just fight for survival and each other. The terror we felt in the darkness that night as we lay there waiting for the battle to begin would become another memory in our never-ending war.

As the night slowly passed, we suddenly began to hear several voices mumbling and a lot movement walking through the bushes behind us at a quick pace. We could hear their equipment making a noise like bamboo hitting against each other as they shuffled along. Even though we could not tell how many there were, we estimated it was a platoon of them, and they were within yards of us. I figured they were pumped up on drugs and adrenaline from the whipping they'd taken from second platoon, and now they were ready to play a little payback on any marine they ran into along the way. Right now, it looked like they were about to run straight into us. At times like this, you realize how painful fear really is. Being certain they would smell the massacre and stop long enough to check out the scene, we all felt like dead men. Suddenly, the noise stopped, and we thought they might be quietly slipping up toward us in the darkness. That's when I had my first panic attack. My breathing became heavy and rapid as the sweat began pouring off me. I began feeling the terror of dying. My first thought was self-preservation, escape. Dig a hole, get in it, and cover up. Everyone will be dead in a few minutes, and no one will ever know what really happened. I took a deep breathe and fought back the cowardly thought of leaving my men and hiding myself in the dirt. As I continued taking deep breaths and exhaling them uncontrollably, my next thought was to just crawl out into the darkness. They'll all be dead, and no one will ever know.

Again thinking "I can't do that. I'm the squad leader, and they're all depending on me," I continued to lie there in the darkness, waiting for the end to begin. My final thought was, "We're all going to die, and there's nothing we can do but kill as many of them as we can before they overrun us." Suddenly, a feeling of great peace came over me dispelling all my fear and dread. My only conclusion was that I must have accepted death and now I was ready to fight. I wasn't afraid anymore.

We spent the next hour or so staring out into the darkness, waiting for the NVA to appear and the battle to begin. They never showed up.

The Night Ends

As the sun finally began coming up, the morning light was ending a night of suspense and terror. Rudisell and I stepped out of the ambush position and walked down the little path that ran beside our ambush site. We could see where they had crossed the road only about twenty yards behind us. We all knew we had survived the night of fear and death, and we were relieved. We only had one causality, and I had caused that one. McDaniels was limping around as we laughed at his dilemma. He would get a purple heart, and no one would have to know how he got it.

Lieutenant Bowen and the second squad came down to our ambush site to view the bodies and congratulate us on our success. First squad joined us, and we talked about how the large group of NVA must have walked right between our ambushes without ever seeing us. It was a miracle they hadn't, and I knew my dad must have been praying for us. We talked big about how we could have gotten a lot more of them if they had walked up on us, but we were all glad we didn't have to fight anymore that night. We then realized that silencing the enemy soldiers was one of the reasons the larger force had not discovered us in the last couple hours of the night. I also felt a little better about myself

★★★

when I found out that I wasn't alone in thinking about saving my own skin—we all had. The important thing was that we stuck together, and in the end, we were ready to fight to the death for each other. That's what marines are trained to do. When we get to the point where we cannot think anymore, our training takes over, and we push through the hard times.

After McDaniels was medevaced out, we packed up and headed north to join up with the company. When we got back to the tanks, we were shocked at what they had gone through that night. Those in second platoon looked like they had been through a windstorm of terror.

No one, including the tankers, were talking, and everyone seemed shaken to the bone. It was obvious that they had won the victory, but the losses they had taken in the process could not be imagined. There were piles of NVA soldiers that had died trying to climb over their fallen comrades and get to the marines inside their perimeter.

I found out through talking to some of the second platoon marines that earlier on the afternoon before, Intelligence (S-2) had gotten word that Kilo Company would be hit by a battalion of NVA that very night. Most companies of battle tanks would have taken off for C-2 before nightfall, but Capt. Mike Wunsch had chosen to keep his tanks out in the bush to help Kilo Company with the impending danger. Captain Wunsch was supposed to rotate home in a matter of days, but he was one of the first ones to die while sitting on top his tank with Lieutenant North (Blue).

They were watching through the tanks night vision scope as enemy troops were trying to find the trip flares the marines had set out earlier in the day. As Lieutenant North was about to step off the back of the tank to warn his men of the impending assault, an RPG round came slamming into Mike's tank, killing him and blowing North off the back. The tankers had told the grunts that if attacked, they would take care of everything. They had their big guns loaded with beehive rounds, and they would throw up a wall of deadly darts and pellets at the enemy when they attacked. The plan would have worked great had it not been hot and muggy that night. The tankers got out of their steel monsters and slept on the top where it was cooler but more dangerous. The sudden attack happened so quickly that many tankers were caught completely off guard. Without warning, two tanks were suddenly on fire and lighting up the grunts' fighting positions nearby. Dazed and wounded from the tank explosion, Lieutenant North was lying on the ground in the open when L/Cpl. Randy Herrold climbed out of his M60 gun hole and found him. He then dragged the lieutenant back to his fighting hole. Herrold began firing his machine gun as the NVA began sweeping up the hill in waves. They were firing a barrage of mortar and RPGs ahead of their attacking troops.

The NVA mortar fire was shifting to the west side of the marines' perimeter, and the attack would soon be following. If the marines could not stop them with their small arms fire, hand-to-hand combat would come next.

Herrold's machine gun was about all that was keeping the gooks from breaking through the marines' perimeter as North climbed out of the safety of the fighting hole and tried to get to a radio. He was wounded for the second time within a half hour as Herrold drug him back to the hole again. Amazingly, Lieutenant North had reached the infantry phone on the back of a tank and directed their deadly fire at the enemy attackers. The tank commander rotated his turret, fired, and annihilated the wave of assaulting troops. The NVA were shocked and fell back. They regrouped and again fired a volley of mortar and RPGs in preparation for the next assault. Herrod's machine gun and the other grunts returning fire broke off the second attack.

The Assault Ends

An AC-47 gun ship, Puff the Magic Dragon, had been summoned by Captain Goodwin and arrived on scene to begin raining death from the sky to break the third and final attack of the
night. The line held, but it came with a cost. The marines suffered
seventeen killed or wounded with the tankers taking the worst of
it because they had been the prime target. In the morning light,
the grunts found their listening post had been over run. They also
found the body of Pfc. Frank Coulombe who had been killed by
a burst from an AK47 along with his team mates who were seriously wounded.

The NVA died in heaps from the tank fléchette beehive
rounds along with machine gun and small arms fire. Herrold told
me later that when he counted the boxes of fired cartridges from
his M60 that night, he'd fired over two thousand three hundred
rounds through his machine gun. It was probably the wildest
night he had ever lived through in his eighteen-year-old life. The
same could be said for the rest of the company's young marines.

The surviving NVA had melted back into the bush before day-
light to fight again. Amazingly, some of them had come within
twenty yards of our ambush site. We were all glad we had survived
the night of death in Leatherneck Square, but we all somehow
knew the events of that night would become painfully engrafted
into our minds as it became part of our own never-ending war.

The undamaged tanks towed the ones that could not move on
their own and put thermite grenades into the two tanks that had
been destroyed. Captain Wunsch was on his last mission with
his tankers before rotating home. He didn't have to be there but
wanted to be with his men one more time. First platoon boarded
the tanks heading back to C-2 artillery base, while second and
third platoons stayed to finish up business around the battlefield.
Kilo Company moved on.

The Battle at the Riverbed

On August 11, 1969, Kilo Company was once again conducting a search-and-destroy mission west of C-2 Artillery Base in the Northern I Corps area of South Vietnam. We'd been out in the bush for about ten days and had only seen small and sporadic fire fights up until then, but this day would be different.

Staying Focused

With the enlisted men not always being informed as to what our specific mission was, we remained conscious of the fact that we were in enemy territory. A fire fight, booby trap, or ambush could erupt at any second, keeping us on alert all the time. It was the only way to be safe in this kill-or-be-killed world we were living in. Unbeknown to us at the time, the constant state of readiness we maintained would be a leading factor in our never-ending war that we would have to battle for the rest of our lives.

The Patrol

Kilo Company had begun forming up to move out at seven in the morning. It wasn't long before the sun began beating down on us with the temperature moving upward of one hundred degrees. The only relief we had from the scorching sun was from a slight breeze blowing from the south, making it almost bearable as our column slowly trudged through the high grass and rolling hills we were patrolling in.

A New Day Begins

As we began to move out, we had to once again shake ourselves back to the reality of war. It seemed that in the times between battles, we had to fight complacency from periods of boredom and lethargy. We'd sometimes get hot and tired from the daily drudgery of breaking brush and simply let our guard down by thinking about home and family. In order to keep our senses sharp, we'd have to continually remind each other to "stay alert, keep your eyes open, and spread out." Unnecessary talking, laughing, slapping biting bugs, or anything else that made a noise was avoided. Once we started to move quietly through the bush, we would have to find the enemy before he found us. This was a war zone, and the meat grinder was no place to become careless.

A Common Trait

It has been noted throughout history that most returning combat veterans tend to develop and share a common character trait. They seem to have become soft-spoken men that are generally perceived to have a greater degree of humility. It may not be humility at all. It could be they learned to talk softly in combat in order to stay alive. That is not to say they won't shout at times, but generally speaking, they had to learn to control their tone of voice so they would not be heard by the enemy. It was a habit they never got out of.

As the company of 180 marines moved quietly through the grasslands, the column spread out for quite a long way by leaving a space of ten feet between each man. We did this to prevent clustering up and making ourselves a better target for some enemy soldier with an automatic rifle.

Our second platoon led by Lt. Oliver North stepped off taking point position with third platoon, Lt. Richmond O'Neill, following in behind. Next came Captain Goodwin's antenna farm of radio operators and then last was first platoon, commanded by Lt. Eric Bowen, bringing up the rear security and outside flankers.

At nine in the morning, after moving through an area of chest-high grass, we crossed over a dried-up riverbed about twenty feet wide with six feet high walls on both sides.

As the last platoon was crossing the stream bed, we heard a lone shot ring out. Someone shouted, "Sniper!" We hit the deck and began scanning the tree line for the hidden assailant before he could fire another round. It sounded like it had come from up front of the column. The radio cracked out for Lieutenant North to move his platoon forward and find the elusive shooter. The rest of us were told to hold our position and stay alert. The tension mounted as we began to sense it might not be just a lone sniper. It seemed to be something bigger going on around us, but we weren't sure what. Minutes later, another shot rang out from a different direction. The third platoon was ordered to "get up and go find the second shooter," leaving first platoon by itself. We should have realized they were separating our platoons so they could attack us separately, but we didn't, and they accomplished their first goal.

We were to soon find out that we had walked into a company of sappers—enemy combat engineers that were coming across the DMZ to create havoc with their explosives in the southern bases. They were fresh, motivated troops with brand-new Chinese equipment, and they were itching to use them on us.

Without warning, the NVA launched their attack on all three of our platoons at the same time. Our first platoon, third squad was sitting on a little knoll on the south side of the canal. I was talking to Doc Jerry Hrzic and showing him a scar on my finger, telling him that it was the only one I was planning to take home with me. As we talked, a sudden crack of an AK47 split the air around us; and without thinking, I tucked my feet underneath me and tumbled forward, sitting up a couple of feet from where I'd been. Looking up, I saw three NVA soldiers standing just above the canal, no more than thirty yards from us. I quickly took aim for the one in the middle, fired one shot to his neck, and dropped him in his socks. The second and third shots I fired took care of his buddies on each side of him. I heard Doc Hrzic behind me counting them as they fell. I was so busy trying to find more of them to eliminate I failed to see that Jerry had been shot twice in the opening burst of rifle fire by the ones I'd just killed. Jerry began immediately trying to patch up his own wounds as I tried to crawl over to help him out, he shouted at me, "I'm okay. Go, go, go!"

Not knowing what else to do, I turned again to the field behind us. I lay down on the mound of dirt and put my full attention on spotting other enemy troops that were attacking us from the rear. The enemy soldiers were staying hidden as they crawled low in the high grass behind us, throwing Chinese grenades by the hands full.

Jerry was hit for the third time with shrapnel from a grenade as he began working on the wounded around him. One grenade came whizzing at me from my left. I jumped up and dove to my right to avoid the blast. It exploded just as I hit the ground. My flak jacket caught several small fragments of shrapnel, but it saved my life by keeping me unscathed. The concussion from the grenade felt like someone had drop-kicked me in my left side, but it drew no blood so I crawled away.

The Canal

Staff Sergeant Landrum began hollering, "Everyone, get in the canal for cover!" So I got up and followed his order like everyone else. Once inside the dried-up canal, we got up against the north wall and discovered that it was too deep to see over. The NVA could walk right up to the edge and throw grenades into the canal on top of us. I shouted to the staff sergeant, "We need to get out of here! It's a death trap!" My words apparently didn't register to him because he continued ordering us to stay where we were. I wanted to get out of the ditch and go back up to the top of the knoll, but it didn't seem to be a real safe option. Pausing in the canal, I didn't know what else to do. Not thinking clear in a moment of chaos, I took off running past the staff sergeant as he shouted, "You're going to get yourself killed!" My immediate thought in passing him was, "It won't be in this ditch!" I had to be able to see the enemy before I could shoot him, and being in the canal didn't give me that opportunity. My action wasn't bravery at all. It was simply common sense and desperation.

On the Mound Again

Once getting back on top of the knoll and lying down to conceal myself in the short grass, I was able to see anyone moving out in front of us. Doc Hrzic was still lying in the same place on the hill as he was trying to stabilize one of our new guys, Pfc. Corkey Cortill who had been shot in both knees. He squinted his eyes and clenched his teeth as he fought back the pain. He kept saying, "I've only been here for a week, and look at me—I'm ruined."

Life, as he'd always known it, had suddenly ended with a crack of a rifle, and now he'd be crippled for the rest of his life. Pfc. Richard Grisson was then brought over to us. A grenade had landed on top of his pack. As he grabbed the small bomb and tried to throw it back, it blew up! The explosion vaporized his right arm, leaving only a six-inch stub from his armpit. As he ran past me, I could see the bone and veins hanging out of the bloody stump. His face was red and twisted from anger, pain, and delirium at the shock of what had just happened. It was a miracle that the grenade hadn't blown his head off as well, but his immediate concern was that his right arm was now and forever missing.

Corpsmen Up

Corpsmen Bill Rister and Hrzic were trying to hold him down and put an IV in his other arm to keep him from going into shock. He was screaming, "Look at what they did to me! My wife will hate me like this!" A quickly assembled medevac position was set up just behind me, so I saw most of the guys they were bringing up to be choppered out. One of the marines in my squad, L/Cpl. Larry Renfro, was brought up to the medical area. A grenade had blown up in his face, ripping his top lip almost completely off and cutting his face up. Only by the grace of God had he escaped being killed by the explosion. Most of the seventeen wounded were taken to a bomb crater first, and once they were stabilized, they were then moved to the medevac position where I was located.

Air Support Comes

Capt. Paul Goodwin immediately summoned air support, and the F4 Phantoms had arrived and were diving in for their bomb run. Lieutenant O'Neill had thrown a purple smoke grenade in the target area to mark the spot where the napalm was to be dropped. One of the fighters that had been circling our position disappeared behind a small hill to our front and, a couple of seconds later, came zooming over the horizon. I had a sudden feeling of terror that his napalm might be dropping on top of us. As the bomb exploded, it was close enough for us to feel the heat but just far enough away not to hit us. As for me, burning to death was not a preferred way of dying.

The exploding fire bombs set the high grass on fire, taking away the camouflage from the enemy. It was fight or flight for the

NVA as some of them tried to run from the battlefield. We killed several that were attempting to get away and all of them who'd stayed behind to fight. The jellied gasoline napalm gave off a terrible stench from the burning fuel and scorched human bodies. The air was permeated with the smell of death, gunpowder, and torn-up flesh as the battle continued on for another two hours.

Back on the Knoll

As I continued to scour the area in front of me for any movement, I spotted an NVA soldier in the high grass, kneeling against a tree about two hundred yards from us. I could have used my rifle to shoot him, but because Pfc. Bob Snyder was kneeling next to me with his M79 grenade launcher, I decided to be different and use that. We laughed at the possibility of me hitting the target at such a long distance as Bob handed me the weapon. I lifted it to my shoulder, aimed a few feet above my target, and fired. We watched the explosive round traveling through the air like a baseball. It missed the soldier but hit the tree only inches from his head. *Blam!* Several marines around us were looking when the round detonated blowing half of the guys head off. Everyone including our wounded started cheering and saying, "Man, what a shot!" It had been one in a million, and I'd pulled it off. The enemy soldier thought he had gotten away, but he hadn't. There is a rule in combat that says, "When your enemy is in range, so are you." Don't take anything for granted as he should have kept running.

Mental Hardness

I'd reached a point where I didn't care about anyone other than the guys in our company. I was starting to lose my emotions. I even had to push myself to write Dad and Paul because I couldn't think of anything worth writing about. There was no meaning to life any longer, and death was just a consequence of living. We all had to die some time.

Misguided Amusement

It was always amusing to us when the enemy got mutilated or physically messed up, but it wasn't so funny when our guys got hit, killed, or lost limbs. We would get mad and go looking for more NVA to take it out on. I don't think God created us to hate like this war was making us to feel. I had ultimate contempt for the Vietnamese people.

Doc Hrzic was still helping put IVs in other marines when they put him on the chopper. The doctor onboard had to make him quit helping others and lie still so they could work on him. Doc Hrzic was a good guy that we could always depend on. He was one of our best corpsmen. Once he left us that day in such a hurry, I didn't know if I'd ever see him again. It would be thirty-eight years before we would accidentally meet again at a 3/3/3 Marine Corps reunion in Orlando, Florida, in 2008. Neither of us had ever been to a reunion before, but we just happened to go to the same one at the same time. Not only did I see Jerry at the reunion, we got up with Mike Mucyn, Tom Rudisill, Wayne "Reb" Williams, Doc Bill Rister, and B. J. Miller. It was an unbelievable experience for all of us. Who would have ever thought we all meet again at the same time.

While there, Jerry gave me one of the greatest compliments I've ever received. He repeatedly thanked me for saving his life at the riverbed that day. The only thing I could say was, "I wasn't trying to stop the gooks from killing you. I was trying to keep them from killing me." We both laughed. Later on that night, the thought occurred to me that if I'd done anything to protect one of our corpsmen, it was good. There couldn't have been anything done on the battlefield more important than helping one of those guys because they were so vital to us grunts. They kept a lot of us from dying out there in the dirtiest and most unsanitary conditions imaginable. They were indispensable in our violent world of mayhem and death. Our navy corpsmen wore the same camouflage utilities as us so they would blend in and not stand out, keeping the enemy from targeting them as valuable targets.

Doctors back in the States did not usually operate on their family members because of the trauma that came with watching your loved one die on the operating table. In the bush, the corpsmen ate, slept, suffered, and fought alongside a bunch of young marines, and we became family. Our docs tried to save the lives of their best friends and, many times, watch them slip away in spite of all they did to save them. We loved and protected our corpsmen.

A Shocking Find

During the battle at the riverbed, as the choppers came in to pick up our medevacs, they dropped nets to put the confiscated NVA equipment and weapons into. They would take them back to our battalion headquarters so we wouldn't have to carry them with us. It was amazing how new the enemy's equipment was compared to the worn-out stuff we had to make do with. The Marine Corps was known to be tightfisted with their money, and most of our equipment were handed down to us from someone who was rotating back home. We'd use seized NVA backpacks because they were bigger and better than the ones we were issued. As we were throwing the enemy gear into the net, I picked up a new AK47 with a brass plate on its stock that read Donated by the same American university. My face turned red as I thought of the fight we had just come through and the ripped-up marines and corpsmen who had just been sent to the hospital and morgue.

We knew the NVA were playing mind games with us, but we also knew that same university was sending money to the NVA to buy food and medical supplies as a humanitarian gesture. The plates on the rifle stocks were just flaunting the fact that they were also using the donations to buy weapons to fight us with. It made us feel like no one was on our side any longer. The NVA were trying to kill us, and our countrymen were supplying them with weapons to do so. This was the second time we'd found those plates on equipment belonging to the NVA.

Unknown to Doc Hrzic, he returned home and later attended that same university to study microbiology. He didn't find out about the rifle plates until 2008. He had studied alongside the ones whom had financed the enemy with weapons to kill him.

A lot of Vietnam veterans never went back home after they had rotated. They chose to live in communes made up of other Vietnam veterans in Washington State, Oregon, and one of the uninhabited islands of Hawaii. They turned their backs on society because they felt society had turned their backs on them. I felt the hate whelming up inside me as I questioned if I really wanted to go back home. If it hadn't been for Dad and Paul, I don't think I would have returned either. We moved on that day to finish up the patrol, ending up at the Rock Pile a couple weeks later. We'd be at the base for three to five days to rest and resupply before moving out again. Those stationed at the base looked at us like we were vagabonds as our company would exit the bush and enter into civilization again. Our sun-bleached uniforms were torn and bloodstained as we appeared to be unkept and smelling bad, but that was all part of the game. We were proud to be Marine Corps grunts.

Rest for the Weary

Whenever we would be at one of the fixed bases for any length of time, it would be a little easier on us mentally, but those places were still in the meat-grinder, and we were never really safe. We had to always be aware of everything around us and stay close to a bunker in case of a sudden rocket or mortar attack. There was never a dull moment in the meat grinder. Wherever we went, we always had to stay proactive and run ambushes, patrols, listening post at night, observation post during the day, and killer teams at night. We had to constantly and consistently pursue the NVA, or they would attack and destroy us. I'm not sure when it hit me, but somewhere along the way, the bush became my home. It was dirty, hot, nasty, and dangerous, but it was home to the grunts, and nobody complained. When we confiscated the enemy's equipment like belt buckles, suspenders, helmets, lighters, and anything else that had a star on it representing North Vietnam, we would sell it to the POGs, people other than grunts, in the rear area. They would come home, looking like a bunch of heroes while we just wanted to come home and be left alone. We would always remember our buddies whom we'd lived and suffered with while out in the bush. That was where we had been tested in the harshest of ways and came out on the other side tempered like steel. We were battle tough, and we could take anything including the job of fighting our enemy face-to-face. The only thing that mattered to me was surviving another day in the meat grinder and hope I didn't let my buddies down in the heat of battle. Everything in our Vietnam experience was working to create our own never-ending war, PTSD.

The Find

In mid-August while operating on an extended long-range patrol west of C-2 artillery base, we began moving into an area of flatland with very low vegetation. In it were one acre sections of ground surrounded by two feet high, four feet wide dikes that had the appearance of an abandoned rice paddy. This kind of abandoned irrigation system reminded us of the battle of Mai Loc. The bushes and weeds on top of the dikes had been unrestrained for some time but still had not grown as high as the ones at Mai Loc. In spite of the plant life being shorter, it still provided an abundance of camouflage and cover for anyone who wanted to take a shot at us.

Kilo Company Marines had to once again spread out over a large area in order to present a smaller target for any would be sniper. They might be able to get one marine, but the others around him would be on the shooter within seconds with deadly response.

As we slowly trudged along through the dried-up rice paddy looking for any signs of the NVA, the word was passed between the men to take five, a short rest. We welcomed the break because of the extreme heat, the humidity, and the eighty pounds of gear we always carried. Whenever we stopped long enough sit down, we simply leaned backward and let the weight of our packs pull us to the ground. We just flopped up against the dike we had been walking beside. It made a good backrest and gave us some protection as we sat there.

As I shifted the weight of my gear and dropped down to the ground, I immediately felt something sharp stick into my upper leg. I squirmed for a second as I thought of it being a stick or rock. When I looked closer, it turned out to be a well placed

60-mm. mortar round hidden in the weeds. A couple of marines on either side of me saw what I'd found and started helping to pull back the thick bushes from around the dike. To our surprise, we soon discovered a dozen or so mortar rounds lying side by side beneath the grass. We continued digging through the weeds until we came across a 60-mm. mortar tube and base plate for the deadly weapon. This was a treasure find because the NVA would have possibly used it against us before we had left the area. We'd robbed them of a valuable piece of small artillery they would have used against the grunts.

We gathered everything up and took it to our lieutenant, showing him what we'd found in the high grass we'd been walking beside. We then carried it over to our 60-mm. mortar team so they could put it into use against our adversary. Our mortar team used the tube to hail deadly mortars at the NVA until our battalion was pulled out of Vietnam in October 1969. It made us feel good that not only had we found the mortar tube, but it was being used on the very ones who had hid it. They would never again be killing or wounding another marine with this weapon, ever again. That was very cool.

The Ongoing War

While searching every day for the elusive enemy, it became evident to us that even though we had won many battles, we never seemed to be making any progress. We would patrol an area like this, looking for NVA activity and ending up in a firefight where we would sometimes kill a lot of enemy combatants. In the process of fighting the NVA, we also took quite a few casualties ourselves. We would then move on to a new area, never claiming any terrain as our own.

In 1969, Kilo Company would go to Mutter's Ridge three times. Each time we went, we would take all the hills on the ridgeline from the enemy, and then, we would leave and go some-where else.

At Mai Loc, we had fighting hours where we could not engage the enemy from sunrise till sunset, 06:00–18:00. We never stayed anywhere long enough to claim territory. I guess we all knew that we were not there to win the war, only to act as a block-ing force to stop the communist aggressors that were coming into South Vietnam. The North Vietnamese, on the other hand, considered us invaders of their country. They did not include the DMZ on any of their maps because they never acknowledged the four-mile wide buffer zone dividing the country into two parts. Statistics would show over fifty-eight thousand Americans died during the war, compared to the more than one million enemy soldiers we killed, but it would go down in history as "America losing the war." The only way the NVA could have won that war was to outlast us. They knew that we were running out of support from our politicians, colleges, and the American media. If they could hold out long enough, they could win no matter how many men they lost.

Americans fighting the war had the will to fight and win, but by 1969, our country had lost their determination to continue the war any longer. They were tired of it. President Richard Nixon had started to create a plan of withdrawal called de- Vietnamzation. A unit size withdrawal from Vietnam that would eventually turn the country over to the South Vietnamese Army. Everyone who knew anything about the war was aware that the SVA was so infiltrated with communist soldiers and sympathizers that they could never protect and defend the South from the invading North by themselves. If we ever pulled out of Vietnam, the South would fall within a few days.

Just a few years later, in 1975, we watched on television the *Fall of Saigon*, which was the culmination of the fall of Vietnam. What we thought would happen actually did. We would be the first American soldiers to return home from a war we had lost.

It was too much shame for many Vietnam veterans to handle as they secluded themselves from the society that had defamed them. It would become an open wound in the heart of many veterans as they became a victim to their own *never-ending war*.

Uncommitted

During the year of 1969, the life of America's fighting men was becoming more difficult by the day. A deadly combination of the turmoil back home and the terror of combat coupled with the misery of being in the bush for weeks and sometimes months at a time made it a daily struggle to stay motivated. Many times it took all the perseverance and dedication we could muster up just to keep from quitting on the mission or your fellow marines.

There were inevitably some who after only being in the bush for a short time would find that this was not what they had signed up for and would look for a quick way out.

They would sometimes make a terrible, uncalculated mistake that would get them back home but end up causing them misery and shame for the rest of their lives.

On one such occasion, first platoon received a couple of BNG.s about the time we were heading up into the hill country outside of Vandergrift combat base. With the temperature seldom dropping below one hundred degrees and having to carry the eighty pounds of gear up and down hills, it was hard on everyone. We were aware that no one was a superman, and we all had to push ourselves to not quit when the going got tough. We didn't need anybody dropping out on us whenever they felt like it. That's not what marines do.

Misguided Intentions

We really frowned on hearing a new guy talk about hurting himself to get out of the bush, and when Pfc. Jeffrey West came to third squad, he started openly whining and complaining right away. We told him to keep his mouth shut and just do his job.

We'd help him get adjusted to his new obstacles, but after only a few days of struggling in the Bush, he informed me that he was going to shoot himself in the foot and go back home.

It made us all mad to hear him dropping out on us because he had just arrived in country, and we needed every gun and everyone to pull together. It seemed like there were always too few of us out in the bush anyway, and we couldn't afford to lose anyone else especially to a self-inflicted wound. As his squad leader, I intentionally thwarted his plan by taking his M16 (.223 caliber) rifle away and giving him a M79 grenade launcher. I was pretty sure he wasn't going to blow himself up just to get out of the bush. The M79 used two types of ammunition. The main one was an explosive type round that had to travel through the air for several meters before it would arm itself to explode. The other was a nasty little beehive round that had a dozen or so ball bearings inside it along with a fiberglass end cap that added to it a shrapnel effect. It simulated a very large double aught shotgun shell that also threw glass at you. The gun barrel was so large it created a particular sound when fired, giving it the nickname Blooper. You did not want to get hit by that thing as it would rip a man apart. After a few days had passed, I sent him and two other marines outside the perimeter on a nighttime listening post. I hadn't thought anymore about him hurting himself after our talk a couple days earlier, thinking he had gotten the message.

Sometime during the night, the platoon radioman woke me up and told me that I had a wounded man on my listening post. The two men with him were bringing him back into the perimeter to be treated. He told me that I needed to find out what had happened out there because there had been no contact with the NVA and the lieutenant wanted to know what went wrong.

As they brought him in, Gunnery Sergeant Bedell came over to us and knelt down behind the head of Private First Class West. I was at his feet, looking at the remains of his wounded and disfigured right foot.

★★★

Realizing that West didn't know the company gunny was listening, I tried to tell him to keep his mouth shut, but he couldn't hear me for moaning. He began his open confession by saying, "I didn't mean to do it. I'm sorry. I didn't know this was going to happen." I looked at him and the gunny and thought, *Oh, well!* The gunny looked at me and nodded as if to say, "Keep talking." I went ahead and started asking him how he had managed to blow his foot off.

He commenced telling me that he had taken a beehive round and pried the hard honeycomb cap off the end of it. He poured all the ball bearings out and then placed *one* pellet back inside the shell. He then popped the end cap back on the projectile. He thought there was only going to be a single ball bearing shot through his foot, and he would be on his way back home. He put the gun muzzle up to his right foot instep and pulled the trigger. *Bloop!* In the darkness, he suddenly realized the devastating consequences of not considering the hard glass end cap shattering and ripping off anything in front of it. In an instant, the only thing left of his foot was his heel. Everything else was gone. Upon hearing this, the gunny flew into a rage as he attacked him, slapping and cursing him to no end. The gunny said he would make sure the private first class would be court-martialed and dishonorably discharged for his self-inflicted wound. He would have to live with his horrible mistake for the rest of his life. There would also be no financial compensation for his loss of limb injury. The gunny stomped off to report to the lieutenant his findings. I sat down beside West and didn't know what else to say except, "Dude, you messed up!"

He lay in the dirt and wept being in utter misery and humiliation. A medevac chopper came in for Private First Class West at sunrise, and we never heard from him again. We all learned some valuable lessons that night about common sense and commitment to our company and our buddies out in the bush. Some mistakes are irreversible, and his had been one.

Monsoon

The monsoon season in Vietnam ran from June to late August, and we stayed wet a lot of the time. When most veterans remember the rainy season in Southeast Asia, they think of obstacle course–type muddy roads; miserable, stinking compounds; or rain-soaked bases where they had to endure the rust, mildew, and mold in their living quarters and equipment until the season was over.

For the unfortunate men who lived in the bush during the wet season, their recall for the time of monsoon was a little different from most others. The marine grunts didn't use tents to sleep in because they were heavy to carry, cumbersome to set up, and downright dangerous to be inside when the enemy was all around us. We figured it was better to be wet than dead, and in order to be safe, we had to sleep in the open near our water-filled foxholes so we'd be ready to fight in a moment's notice. The only covering available to us in those days was a government-issued poncho, a five-by-five-foot piece of plastic with an attached hood for your head to stick through. We could either wear it, tie the four corners to nearby trees and make a shelter, make a lean-to, or button two ponchos together to make a tent.

On a Cold and Rainy Mountain Top

It was already dark when we stopped patrolling for the night, and the temperature was dropping quickly. It was normally so hot we could hardly breathe, but being so high up on the mountain and in a rainstorm at that, it started to get cold. We couldn't dig a fighting hole in the dark, so Renfro, Ritchie, and I lay down in the rain-soaked mud, and the three of us covered up with one

★ ★ ★

poncho. It was a tight squeeze, but we soon stopped shivering. As we were just starting to warm up, I jokingly told Renfro that the back of his head reminded me of my girl friend. We all started quietly laughing. Renfro then told Ritchie and me to get away from him before he shot both of us. We continued laughing anyway. Even in the middle of this crummy situation of rain, cold, and mud, we still found something to laugh about. We were a band of brothers. Our bed was the wet ground, and it was amazing how comfortable I could get while lying in water so long as I didn't move. At the slightest movement, a sudden surge of chill would cover me, and I'd shiver even more. As hard as we tried, it was impossible to stay motionless because we had to sit up on watch next to our fighting hole every third hour throughout the night. Along with the normal interruptions, there was also an occasional itch or leg cramp to keep me from getting too comfortable as I lay in my natural water bed waiting for the night to end.

Wet Feet

Living with wet boots became the norm, and no matter how soaked our feet became, we never took our boots off after it got dark. If a sudden firefight erupted during the night, we wouldn't have time to find and put them on in the middle of a battle. I tried to carry an extra pair of socks to change nightly, but they only stayed dry until I put my wet boots back on. My feet stayed wrinkled and sore all the time. Our corpsmen kept watch on us as some men even got trench foot from their feet being wet for so long a time during the monsoon season. There was no way to escape the weather when you lived in the bush.

Standard-Issued Gear

Most of us had ponchos that we could put on during a sudden rainstorm, but they would still get us drenched from our sweat and high humidity of the tropics. It was sometimes more tolerable and cooler to not wear them at all and go ahead and get wet. When stopping for the night, we would take off the poncho and tie the corners to nearby tree limbs to use them for a cover from the frequent monsoon rainstorms. At other times, the rain would come down so hard it would create a whiteout situation causing us to lose contact with each other as we walked in a column. We'd have to stop or take hold of the mans pack in front of us so we wouldn't get separated from the platoon as we moved through the bush. Stopping the column was safer because bunching up in groups would always increase our chances of getting shot by a sniper.

A Miserable Life

After spending an exhausting day patrolling the area, we would have to make our bed on the soaking wet ground for the night. It was wet, but at least, it was soft and spongy. No one complained much, and we just took it in stride as I counted off the days until my rotation date of going back home.

Another problem was the abundance of mosquitoes and leaches. They loved the damp areas as much as we hated them. We had to constantly watch out where we made our bed so we could avoid the slimy, nasty blood-sucking leeches that were seemingly everywhere.

It was comical watching a new guy find his first leech feeding on him as his blood ran from the bite. The marine would slap and beat himself half to death, trying to make the thing let go. We used a lit cigarette or bug spray to make them release their grip.

The high temperature and humidity of the wet season also caused scratches and nicks from the elephant grass to become infected in only a short amount of time. The open sores were aptly called jungle rot. As I sat under a poncho covering during one of the many rain showers, I made a list of things that I'd never take for granted again. It consisted of such things as hot, home-cooked food; soft, clean beds; clean clothes; and hot showers. I can't remember taking any more than six showers during my tour of duty in Vietnam, and most of those were during the time I was sick with malaria. There were no showers in the bush and the fixed bases we occasionally stopped at had no running water. We mainly performed a bird bath whenever possible, and the rain, waterfalls, streams, and sudden rain storms took care of the rest. Staying clean was not our number one concern when living in the jungles of Southeast Asia. The fact was, if we smelled like anything other than dirt, it could cost us our lives. I didn't realize how good I'd had it until certain things were gone out of my life. We lost a lot of conveniences when we came to live in the wilds of this third-world country.

In July 1969, as we had entered into the monsoon season, our battalion headquarters decided to send us up onto the mountain overlooking the east side of the Rock Pile (RP) Artillery Base. The compound had been attacked on several previous occasions with most attacks coming from the mountain beside them. Battalion wanted to know if the NVA were building up any forces in the area to mount a future attack.

Kilo Company pulled out of the Rock Pile compound, and Mike Company took our place manning the perimeter lines around the base. We began a three-day search-and-destroy mission into the hill country to look for the NVA. It was hot, rainy, and humid as we climbed the steep incline up to the top of the small mountain. During the three days of patrolling, we only had sporadic contact with the enemy but saw no signs of a buildup in their forces. After completing our mission, we started descending back down the mountain to the artillery base. About halfway down, we received word that there was a typhoon heading our way, and they projected it hitting us sometime during that night. Because Mike Company had already filled our ranks in the RP compound, there was no room for us to go back to. We were told to return back up to the area we had camped at the night before and hunker down. The weather was going to get worse before getting better, and we had to get prepared for the coming storm. We set up our perimeter again, tied the corners of our flimsy ponchos to nearby tree limbs for cover, and hoped for the best. It was like waiting for a car wreck to happen.

That evening, the typhoon hit just before dark with a fieriness as the winds came over the mountain at seventy-five miles per hour, instantly blowing our poncho coverings down and away. It was blowing a gale as we desperately tried to get under some kind of cover against the elements with very little results showing for our efforts.

We grabbed our ponchos out of the trees and covered up with them as best we could, staying close to the ground to avoid the brunt of the wind. We spent the next ten hours caught outside in a category 1 hurricane with nothing but a flimsy piece of plastic to cover up with. There were three of us marines trying to hold on to and get under one poncho at the same time. It was not pretty at all. Parts of all three of us were hanging outside the poncho as we hung on for dear life in the onslaught of wind and rain. With all the vegetation of a jungle being blown around in a frenzy, we knew it was a volatile situation of not being able to see or distinguish anything or anyone moving around us. We didn't care. We just hoped the enemy was smart enough to lay low until the storm passed and the mayhem ended. They were probably sitting around in a dry tunnel somewhere underneath of us, laughing at our dilemma. We felt really stupid, sitting under a poncho in a hurricane.

More Stupidity

Before the storm had hit, we were told to still take turns standing watch at our fighting holes. At one point in the storm, I peeked from under our poncho covering to see Lance Corporal Grogan sitting in front of our fighting hole with nothing on to cover him from the weather and his feet submerged in the water filled cavity. Talk about dying obedience. I couldn't help but laugh at him as he sat in the torrential downpour.

Early the next morning, the rain moved on, and we surveyed the slight damage we had incurred. Most of the damage was to our pride. We had been beat up all night by a hurricane that slapped us around with the same bushes we were trying to hide under. We packed up our soaking wet gear and started down the mountain once again. Our cigarettes had become one of the first casualties of the storm, and we were dying for a smoke. Ritchey and I found some water logged C ration cigarettes and tried to toast them over a small open flame to dry them out. They were Pall Mall cigarettes that had been packaged in 1944. *Strong* was not the word to describe the taste of them. They were deplorable, but we smoked them anyway.

We ended up at the Rock Pile a few hours later and stayed just long enough to replenish our supplies and then back out into the Bush again. I wrote Dad and told him that everything was okay. I tried to explain to him what it was like living outside the house during a hurricane. It was an experience of a lifetime. He might have thought I was making it up because he knew that no one in their right mind would do such a foolish thing. I suppose it was because he was never in the Marine Corps. Most of what I'd say was small talk and then remind him to keep us in his prayers and send me some presweetened Kool-Aid. I knew that God was keeping me alive, and I did not deserve his favor. My dad must have been putting a good word in for me.

Photos

A grunts best friend.

Doc Hrzic and Ray at the Martial Arts
Hall of Fame induction 2008

★★★

home-sweet-home

Laura and Ray at MS reunion

nighttime in the bush

Parris Island, SC boot camp

★ ★ ★

PFC Clark 1967

Ray and Lt. Haskell at Rolling Thunder

Ray and O. North 2012

Ray Clark: Parris Island 1966

Ray looking at RPG 1969

Rays coping skill #9

Resupply and medivac

Saddle up for patrol

★★★

Taking a 5 min. break

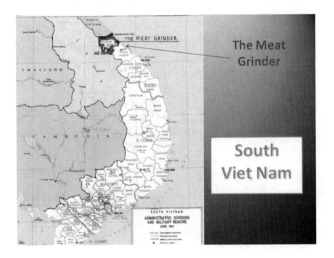

The meat grinder area of Vietnam

The meat grinder

The spoils of the battle

★★★

Victims of war

Walking point in the meat grinder

The Listening Post

In late August of 1969, Kilo Company was finishing up an operation in the Rock Pile area in an attempt to intercept NVA units moving south through the region. The company had separated into three platoon-sized patrols. Each platoon would move as a unit by day and then split up into three squad size ambushes at night.

One afternoon, Lieutenant Bowen received word from the company commander that an NVA Battalion had been located moving into our area with plans of attacking Kilo Company that very night. Captain Goodwin called for all three platoons to suspend their patrols and rendezvous ASAP. We had to coordinate a good defensive position before dark in order to be ready for the impending attack by an overwhelming force. First platoon began heading east immediately, trying to cover several thousand yards of open territory that separated us from the rest of the Kilo Company. Even though we didn't like to hurry when moving through the bush, we had break the rule to make the crossing as quickly as possible to get there before dark.

As we were getting within a few hundred yards of the company's position, we came up on a large field that we had to cross because it was too big to go around.

As we stepped into the field, the grass was chest high, which made it difficult to walk through with the eighty pounds of gear we were carrying. We couldn't even see the ground in front of us as we had to pick our feet up high to step through the tall weeds. The field was so large and open, I had to take the precautionary action of spreading my squad out in a wide semicircle to make us less of a target to any sniper in the area. We were anxious to get through this grassland because it looked like a good place to get

★★★

shot at, and it was our last obstacle before arriving at our company's position. It would also be getting dark in about an hour or so.

We were making good progress in getting through the meadow when suddenly, I put my foot down in front of me, and there was nothing there. I fell straight into a large, deep hole or, rather, a pit. The hole was about three feet wide, five feet long, and six feet deep. The walls were perfectly straight, and it looked like it had been recently dug and for a specific reason. The bottom of the pit was pitch-black, and I couldn't see anything. A sharp stick pierced my leg causing my first thought to be, "I've fallen into a punji pit." Punji stake is a sharpened bamboo stake. The NVA would put several dozen inverted stakes in the bottom of a pit, and when someone fell in, they would be impaled on them. They would also dip them in feces in order to poison their victim for a horrible death.

Suddenly realizing that I was still alive, I quickly ruled out the punji pit theory. My next thought was that it might be a snake pit. I hurriedly got back up on my feet, eighty pounds of gear on, and looked at the pit floor to see if there were any snakes. To my relief, there were none. By this time, my eyes were adjusting to the darkness and allowed me to see clearly again. I could see the sides of the pit had fresh shovel marks in the dirt, and the soil was still wet indicating it had just been dug. I began hollering for someone to come and find me before they moved on out of the area. I heard Pfc. Terry Ruggie say, "Clark, I'm coming." With that, he fell straight into the pit right on top of me. Everyone saw him drop out of sight and came running over to us. A couple of marines handed their rifle stocks down for us to grab onto and pulled us out. From what we hastily surmised, apparently, we had walked up on the NVA while they were possibly making a punji trap. They saw us and took off, leaving the unfinished pit before they could put the stakes in the bottom. If we had been thirty minutes later, there would have possibly been two dead marines in the pit. My mind was spinning as I thought God had saved my life again! I would have to write my dad and tell him about the incident. I'd remind him to keep on praying for me as things were getting more intense every day.

We continued moving on until we reached the company perimeter about a half hour later. Once we were placed into our nighttime perimeter position, we started digging our fighting holes. They would have to be dug right by the book because we knew we would need their protection before sunrise.

Lieutenant Bowen called a squad leaders' meeting, and the three of us joined him at the command post. He told us that S-2 (Intelligence) had informed our company commander that a battalion, four companies, of NVA had been sighted following us. They knew where we were, and they would be attacking us that night. They estimated a one hundred percent chance of us being attacked before morning by a numerically superior force in the darkness. This was definitely *not* good news. We were looking at a three-to-one ratio in their favor. It almost made me sick to my stomach to think about what we were facing. All we could do was dig in and put up a good defense.

This time, we didn't have tanks to help us out, but we did have air cover, and that was our only hope for survival. We would light up the heat tabs in the bottom of our fighting holes, and once again, we'd let Puff do his thing, hoping he didn't over shoot his target and hit us.

During the meeting, Lieutenant Bowen then gave me the bad news. I had to send three men out on a listening post (LP), and they needed to get ready to go out because it was already getting dark. They would have to go out about a 150 yards from our company perimeter and set up their listening post in order to spot the approaching enemy troops.

My thoughts were spinning as I went back to my squad to pick the three men to go out from the safety of our perimeter and hide out in the bush until morning. Their job was to warn the company whenever they detected movement so the perimeter could be alerted and prepared for the attack. The LP could stay where they were and hope they weren't discovered by the enemy, or they could try to run back into the perimeter and risk being shot in the back by the NVA or shot in the front by a nervous marine on the lines. They might even be shot by Puff as they were outside of the lit-up (heat tabs) perimeter.

I couldn't come out and tell them, but neither choice sounded promising for the lives of the three unfortunate volunteers.

My third squad was already aware of the impending battle that was about to take place. When I told them that I needed three volunteers to go out on an LP, they all took one step back and asked me if I knew how many NVA were supposed to show up later. I told them that I did, but we still had to send out a listening post.

I didn't tell them so, but I truly felt that whomever I sent out that night would probably not be coming back alive. The odds were too high against them. We'd never had a one hundred percent chance of a nighttime battle before. This was serious. I wished they would send out a bunch of helicopters and take us out of there, but we were marines, and our superiors would never do that.

Knowing that I could have picked any three of my men and they would have reluctantly gone out did not make the job any easier. The most experienced men knew how the deck was stacked against us, and they really didn't want to go. Taylor whispered to me that I should send the two new guys. We didn't even know their names yet, and it wouldn't matter if they got wasted. We all laughed at the idea, but the new guys didn't think it was funny. They had overheard Taylor talking to me.

As much as I didn't want to hear it, my dad's words kept haunting me about not making someone do what I was too scared to do myself. I sure wished he had never told me that. How could I send three men out to possibly die when I myself was scared and stayed in the safety of our perimeter? I didn't know if I could ever live with myself. Knowing what had to be done, I took a deep breath and made my decision. L/Cpl. Otis Taylor would take over the squad for the night, and I'd take the two new guys out with me. Bravery had absolutely nothing to do with my decision. I just couldn't live with myself for sending my friends out to die while I stayed in relative safety inside our lines. Somewhere along the way, I came to belong to these men, and this way of life. It was hard, dirty, and dangerous, and we would forever be bound by a common thread known as a band of brothers. That's why we were constantly putting our lives on the line for each other. We were family, and we would never fit into society again because this is where we came to belong. These men and times would always be a central part of my life.

I took the squad radio and told L/Cpl. Mike Mucyn and Pfc. Bob Logan to follow me. We walked over to the fighting hole that had the M60 machine gun positioned in it. By the light of the moon, I pointed out to the gun team of Ronnie Thompson and Pfc. Pepper the island of bushes that was about 125 yards away. I told them we would be hiding inside there and we took off.

As we left the perimeter, everyone was looking at us with a gloom-and-doom expression on their faces like we were going on a suicide mission. Thompson said, "You guys be careful out there." I reminded the gun team, "If you see a flare go up, that means we're coming in. Don't shoot! We know where your position is too, and we'll shoot back!" They laughed and said okay as we walked out into the darkness.

Into the Valley of Death

We hurriedly got to the little island of bushes and sat down in the middle of them. I explained to the two new guys that the platoon radioman would call every five minutes and ask for a SID-REPs. We would press the button on the handset twice without speaking, and this would let them know that we were awake and

★ ★ ★

everything was okay. We would stay on watch for one hour each, starting with Mucyn, then Logan, and then me. We rotated like this for the rest of the night. I told them while on watch that if they heard, smelled, or saw anything at all, no matter how small, to quietly wake me up, and I'd decide whether we would hunker down and stay there, or we'd try and make it back to our lines. They both assured me they understood the seriousness of what was expected of them. Mucyn took the first watch, and Logan and I went to sleep.

Mucyn told me later that he had never been so scared in his whole life. He knew that they were sent out there because they were new and the others expected the LP to have major problems before morning. Mike said they really thought they were going to die. I replied, "Me too!"

Mentally Drained

Even though we thought we were going to die that night, I slept sound while waiting for my turn to stand radio watch. I must have been physically and mentally exhausted from the anguish of facing death in the darkness. I hardly remember closing my eyes. Mucyn finished up his first hour shift and woke up Logan to begin his. Sometime during his watch, he fell asleep.

The platoon command post inside the perimeter didn't know if we were dead or asleep because no one was answering the radio SID-REPs. Everyone in the company perimeter stayed awake all night long, and no one was brave enough to come out and check on us. They thought we had gotten our throats cut and the gooks were about to attack at any minute.

Morning Comes

The first thing I remember hearing was a bird singing. I opened my eyes, and the sun was up and shining bright. We had slept all night long, thanks to Logan, and I'd gotten my best night's sleep since my bout with malaria. It must have been from the stress of imminent death that helped me sleep so sound. Thanks to my dad's prayers, there must have been angels watching over us too. We could hardly believe we were still alive.

As we returned to the perimeter, Lieutenant Bowen was furious and told me he thought we should have gone out further than what we did. I responded back that I'd gone out over a hundred yards or so and that seemed far enough to me, considering the circumstances. It was obvious by our appearance that we had slept all night, and that probably embarrassed him in front of the other officers. We really hated that. Fortunately for us, the light from a full moon took away the covering of darkness the NVA would have used to slip up on us. They never showed up, and it was all a false alarm. God had simply used the moon light to discourage an overwhelming enemy force from attacking our company.

Amazing Grace!

The other company officers were not impressed with our little sleep over either, but what could they say? The guy fell asleep and did not wake up anyone. He would be punished later, but for now, we were all happy that the enemy had gone somewhere else. My squad thought it was hilarious. We had gone out to die and ended up having a great night's sleep while everyone else in the lines had to stay awake all night. My dad must have been praying for us throughout the night for this to turn out the way it did.

A few days later, we arrived at C-2 Artillery Base. While there, the lieutenant called me into his bunker. He reprimanded me for the sleeping incident and told me that he was not going to write me up on charges. He also said that some didn't think we'd gone out far enough and that someone had called us cowards. That made me mad. I couldn't imagine why those "brave souls" didn't come out there to check on us. I told him about making the decision to take the other two men out that night and we all thought we were going to die before morning. I also reminded him that I'd been recommended for two Bronze Stars for gallantry in the past three months. I didn't get those for being a coward.

Prior Commendations

I'd been recommended for a Bronze Star in the fight at the riverbed. I'd gone against orders to stay in the canal and moved to a better position overlooking the battlefield. I was able to find and kill four NVA soldiers in the process. Someone saw me and thought it was an act of bravery, but there was nothing brave about it. Simply getting out of the canal made good sense to me.

There were two Bronze Stars and one Silver Star awarded in that battle to each platoon. I had been number three in line for the Bronze Star, so I didn't receive one. I didn't care so much about winning medals, but I'd heard that you usually got a promotion with the medal. I wanted the promotion to corporal. The rank was frozen due to so many corporals returning home from Vietnam, and about the only way to get the promotion was by getting a medal.

The other recommendation came after the ambush my squad pulled on the NVA that were carrying their dead buddies. The medal was to be awarded to the squad leader of the ambush team. Once we had gotten back to the rear area, Corporal Rudisill came into the tent where I was and sat down with me. He had a clip board with him and told me that I'd been awarded a Bronze Star. We needed to write up the commendation for the medal. There were prewritten paragraphs of different combat situations that helped us build a commendation to fit our ambush. We talked and laughed about the ambush that night and how we had been so busy trying to stay alive that we really didn't think about who did what or when. It was like a blur in our minds. As we were kidding around, Rudisill jokingly said, "I started to take the medal for myself." I heard him and was puzzled by what he'd said. I asked him what he meant. He said well, "I outranked you, but the medal was designated for the squad leader." I began to think about what he had said. He did outrank me, and he was getting ready to rotate back home. He was going to Parris Island and become a drill instructor, and if he got the star, he would pick up the rank of sergeant. It all looked like a perfect package befitting Rudisill.

He was one of the best marines I'd ever known. I knew there was no way of telling what could have happened had he not helped me in the ambush site that night. I knew he was more deserving of it than me. I told him to go back and see if they would change the recommendation to him instead of me. He said no, but I insisted. He finally agreed to do it. We laughed at the thought of me having plenty of time left to get me another one before rotating back home, especially in the meat-grinder of Vietnam.

A little while later, Rudi came past me, wearing his new sergeant chevrons on his collar. I was glad for him, but hating it for the second time that my dad would never know I'd been awarded the medal. It would have made him proud.

I don't think I've ever done anything in combat for medals or self-glory. If anything turned out right, it was because of desperation, instinct, and training along with being scared to death. Heroes—they who have the most amount of guts usually have the least amount of brains. There is very little difference between bravery and stupidity. Both will get you killed. Most things happen before you can think of the consequences. You just instinctively react. We simply knew that if someone didn't do something quickly, we'd all die. In most circumstances, my squad didn't have to be told anything. They all reacted to the situation and would just go forward, fight, and destroy the enemy without hesitation.

My job was to orchestrate our movements in the bush and make sure they had food, water, and munitions to fight with. They were all good marines that could be counted on when things got tough.

Kilo Company was involved in a lot of combat with the enemy, and we did take a lot of casualties, but we always ended in victory. We were fighting a formidable foe that had been fighting for fifty years in the same place and had adapted to his terrain in every way. No matter what anyone said, the NVA were skilled fighters.

After being in the meat grinder for six months, there had been too many close calls and near misses of dying, and they had started taking a toll on my nerves. It didn't ever stop me from doing my job, but it was becoming clear to me that I had changed and would never be the same person I had been before going to Vietnam. I had become hard and cruel through the constant bombardment of death, fear, anger, and grief. The inhumanity and degradation of life we experienced during our tour of duty would stay with us for the rest of our lives. Our buddies were now brothers for life, and no one could ever duplicate the friendships that were *forged* in combat. The memories and nightmares of that horrid place would be engrafted into our minds, and we would never mentally and emotionally be allowed to leave that place, causing for us our never-ending war.

Last Time at the Rock Pile

On September 1, 1969, Kilo Company returned to the Rock Pile Artillery Base once again to resupply and man the lines for a few days. On our second day there, third squad was told to provide security for a checkpoint at the north gate of the compound. During the early afternoon, I went to check on the three-man fire team that was manning the gate. As we were standing around talking, a big army troop carrier pulled up to the gate coming from the north.

The driver, a Vietnamese enlisted soldier, got out of the truck and walked around the vehicle. He was joined by a Vietnamese officer who jumped out of the passenger side of the truck. The two of them began approaching the marines standing at the closed gate. We met them and asked what they wanted. They began trying to make hand gestures and verbally communicate with Lance Corporal Renfro and Private First Class DeRusso in extremely heavy broken English as Lance Corporal Ritchie and I walked around the truck to see what they might be carrying. The back of the truck had a canvas covering over the bed, so it had to be checked out. We looked inside and found it was empty. Walking back over to where the others were standing, Renfro told me he thought they had come to borrow a 155-mm. artillery piece. I said, "Yeah, right!"

Renfro continued asking them their intent until we realized that was exactly what they wanted to do as crazy as it sounded. We continued asking them questions and watching them closely to find out if they were South Vietnamese or the enemy trying to pull a daring but stupid move. Everything about them looked

★★★

legitimate until Renfro looked at the enlisted man's feet. He was wearing North Vietnamese sandals that were made from truck tire treads. Renfro pointed out the soldiers' footwear to the rest of us as we chuckled about the dumb mistake they'd made.

Now with growing suspicions, we backed away and held them at gunpoint until we could find out more information about them. They didn't argue or protest our actions as they just became real quiet from that point on. I called our command post and reported that we had visitors at the gate and suspected them of being NVA I reported to them that the enemy soldiers had come to borrow a 155-mm. artillery piece from the base. The CP thought I was crazy and said, "No way!" They could hardly believe the enemy would try something like this. They told us to hold them under guard until they could send someone to escort them down to the CP area. A few minutes later, several marines arrived in a jeep, and the two captives were taken off to be interrogated. An hour later, we were told that they had been confirmed NVA soldiers, and they had brazenly come to borrow an artillery piece along with a basic amount of ammunition from us. I guess they were going to return the ammunition later that night by a different means. It was hard to believe they would try such a bold move, and we were glad we'd stayed with our instincts and checked them out. I'm sure they would never have been able to borrow a big gun from the base, but had they been allowed to walk around the compound that day, they could have caused havoc among us by noting all our positions and gun placements. It was good for us that the enlisted man had unthinkingly worn his NVA shoes on this bold mission to make the marines look like idiots. The enemy officer probably wanted to tear his head up for making that stupid mistake. They were now prisoners of war.

I was also told to go the platoon command bunker and pick up the mail for my squad. Along with all the other stuff we received, my dad had sent me a "care package". I couldn't wait to tear into it. There was a carton of Marlboro cigarettes, cookies, candy, and—what do you know—ten packs of presweetened Kool-Aid. Thank the Lord! Mail and packages like this were priceless to all of us. They told us that our families loved and missed us, and we really needed to hear that in this miserable country.

Our New Mission

Later that afternoon, a squad leaders' meeting was called to meet at the platoon command bunker at 17:00. We usually got updates and directions on upcoming operations at these meetings, and we never knew what to expect. Lieutenant Bowen was all excited about something as he was getting ready to break the news to us. He smiled and said, "We're heading back up to the Ridge in two days." Our countenance dropped as the mood changed from light and easy to shock.

He didn't have to say what ridge as we knew exactly what he meant. The infamous Mutter's Ridge. The most combative area in Vietnam. I thought he was going to tell me my squad was going on a killer team patrol that night, but this was the worst news he could have given us. We looked at each other as we shook our head from side to side in a way of saying ,"Oh no! Not again?" The lieutenant had been in Vietnam for three months and had only heard the war stories about the ridge from Ollie North, Captain Goodwin, and Richmond O'Neill. He was visibly and understandably excited about the prospects of going to this place he'd only heard about. He'd been told that there would be plenty of action up there and wondered why we weren't elated too.

Action, Like Fighting and Dying!

We just couldn't get excited about going to the deadliest place in South Vietnam. The riflemen were considered the triggermen in the company, and we would be the ones who'd be doing all the fighting. The peons didn't care about becoming heroes. All our heroes were dead. Even with all the negative comments being talked about the ridge, there were still some that seemed to be overjoyed at the prospects of the adventure ahead of us. The three squad leaders in the meeting had been there before and knew that it was one of the deadliest places in Vietnam. It was on the southern boarder of the DMZ, and there was usually a regiment or so of NVA gathered in the area around Mutter's Ridge.

Lieutenant Bowen said, "We had to go in and find out how many were there and why they were building up their forces." We knew why! They wanted to kill us. The seasoned marines knew this was the enemy's territory, and the NVA were there to do business. If you wanted a good fight, this was the place to go, and they were ready and willing to give you one. Our commanding officer, Col. Paul B. Goodwin (USMC Ret.), had studied the enemy defensive positions and concluded that the NVA positions on Mutter's Ridge were generally organized around heavily camouflaged fighting bunkers, which had thick overhead cover able to deflect anything but a direct hit. It had a narrow firing aperture and a low silhouette that made them almost impossible to see. Knee-high firing lanes were cut in the jungle growth, allowing the defenders to see but not be seen by advancing infantry. The NVA tactics allowed the American troops to get close enough to their positions as possible, so casualties caused by the initial burst of fire could not be recovered, cutting off the use of fire support.

The American commanders would either have to attack head-on in prepared lanes of fire to rescue their wounded or withdraw and call in artillery leaving the wounded to fend for themselves. The terrain on Mutter's Ridge gave the NVA perfect opportunity to utilize that type of tactics on Kilo Company. It could end up in a blood bath, and we might end up on the short end of the stick if we weren't careful.

Facing Another Mission

We came out of the meeting mad, depressed, and unnerved about the coming days and the coming battles that surely lay ahead of us. I asked Cpl. William Bushey what he thought of the upcoming operation. He simply replied, "Clark, I'm rotating home in two weeks, and then I'll be gone. I just have to make it another two weeks. Bill was going to get married when he got back home, and the wedding was all set, just waiting for him to get there." He was excited about that!

During the squad leaders' meeting, I was ordered to take my squad on an ambush that night. Before leaving the perimeter, I told them of the plan to go back to the ridge again. They could hardly believe it. The seasoned veterans knew about the high probability that some of us would not be coming back, and the new guys didn't know what to think. They became upset because the old salts were throwing and kicking things around our bunker. The BNGs didn't know what to think. As their tensions boiled over inside the bunker, I just let them vent until we got to the gate. From that point on, we all shut up and moved out to our proposed ambush site. There was nothing we could do but go when we were told to go. We would have to use all the knowledge and wisdom we had acquired in combat to keep us alive and get the mission accomplished. In our simplistic way of thinking, success in combat was knowing how to kill the enemy without losing any of our own men in the process. Mutter's Ridge was the kind of place where the inexperienced didn't last very long, and I felt sorry for the BNGs we'd just picked up. There was no way they could begin to fathom the danger they were about to face in this place called Mutter's Ridge. New people in country will get killed and get others killed by misjudging or underestimating the enemy. My squad members let me know that they trusted my judgment in the bush, and we would all take care of each other.

We went out that night and set up our ambush in our intended ambush site, but it turned out to be a much less traveled location than what we expected. It worked out to be a good thing because

I knew we all needed to calm down from all the tension and worry we were feeling. I called in our ambush position and settled in for the night as I tried to clear my thoughts about the news we'd been given earlier in the day .

At Sunrise

We had zero contact throughout the night and got up after sunrise. We then moved out in a staggered combat formation back to the Rock Pile compound and back into our bunkers on the perimeter. Everyone looked to be depressed by the appalling news.

Preparing for Battle

Everyone seemed a little quieter than usual, and most were writing letters to their girlfriends, wives, and families. We were not telling our loved ones of the impending danger, but we just wanted to send our love and communicate with someone who cared about us. We could possibly have been writing our last letter, and we wanted to make sure they knew we were thinking about them. After checking our squad members for any items they might need in the upcoming operation, I finally arrived back at my bunker. I paused at the doorway and noticed a *Stars and Stripes* military newspaper lying on a nearby sandbag. The newspaper was a good source of encouraging reading material for the troops to enjoy, which came far and few between. I picked it up and scanned through the pages. Near the back section of the paper was a cartoon that caught my attention. It was a picture of a brand-new officer decked out with spit-shined boots, shiny brass, and wearing a crisply starched uniform. He was walking beside a marine private that was using a crutch to help him stand up. He was wearing shredded utilities, his head was bandaged, and his arm was in a sling. It was apparent the private had been just come through some heavy fighting and was in need of immediate medical attention. The caption at the top read, "Thanks, Private," and the lieutenant was saying, "You did a good job today. I should get me a medal for what you did."

I couldn't help but laugh, but I shouldn't have because it wasn't funny! I think it was my nerves going awry. That kind of situational ethics would not happen where we were heading. Everyone who went to the ridge would have to pull their own weight, and if anyone got a medal, they would have to earn it for themselves. Most officers in Kilo Company tried to lead their men by example, which was Captain Goodwin's first rule of conduct for them. He knew there were some in Vietnam that would volunteer their men for a dangerous mission just to make themselves look good, but his officers would not do that.

Kilo Company officers would not only send us out on a dangerous assignment, but they would lead us. They cared about their men, and we liked to serve under that kind of officer. Kilo Company had a reputation for beings a top notch Marine Corps Rifle Company, and we were proud to be part of it.

September 3, 1969: Operation Idaho Canyon

Word went out on the morning of September 3, 1969, for everyone to saddle up. That meant to put on everything you had and form up in platoons at the north gate of the Rock Pile base. At that moment, no one could possibly know this would be our last time at the Rock Pile Marine Artillery Base. President Nixon's de-Vietnamization program was in the beginning stages and unknowing to many of us, 3/3 was scheduled to be pulled out of the country very soon and be redeployed to Hawaii. Within minutes of getting the word, we started to make the short trek from our bunkers toward the north gate where my squad was immediately put to the lead position of first platoon. We stopped, dropped our gear, sat down, and leaned back against our packs while waiting to get the word to move out. The company lined up in a column with second platoon taking point position, third platoon and the command post next, and then first platoon bringing up the rear position.

> One famous saying in the Marine Corps is to never run when you can walk, never walk when you can stand, never stand when you can sit, never sit when you can lie down, never just lie down when you can sleep, and never pass up a chance to get a fresh supply of clean water.

I always took advantage of every opportunity to get a power nap as we never knew when the next time would come when we'd be able to rest. Throughout the next hour or so of lying back on our packs, it became obvious that a lot of people were joining in with our column. We were glad to see them coming along with us and welcomed them in knowing we'd soon be needing the extra men and firepower they brought along. We found out later on that instead of the normal 180 men in our company, we had elevated our number to a whopping 203 men. This was because a lot of support people had joined in with our company. Battalion headquarters knew we'd need all the elements of support we could get when heading into the DMZ area.

Obvious Stress

The emotions of going into battle could be seen on the faces of all the men. Most of us were between eighteen and twenty years old, but you would have never known it by the level of maturity these guys showed in combat. Being with them was like being on a big hunting and camping trip in the wide-open country. Although in this case, the one great difference was that the hunted were armed and deadly and would be hunting us at the same time. We couldn't allow ourselves to dwell on the danger factor, less the stress and tension of the occasion would make old men out of us quickly. Going out to do combat with an armed opponent creates a heavy burden for anyone to bear. We were supposed to be big bad marines, but the truth was we were all scared of the unknown. Our only resolve to the situation was to face the emanate danger head-on because we couldn't let it stop us from doing our jobs. We laughed about how we were going out to kill people we weren't even mad with. The emotional battle of facing death was something we all were having to overcome on an individual basis, and it was adding heavily to our own never-ending war.

Elements of Support

The extra men that joined up with our company that day included a forward air controller, artillery forward observer, and a dog handler with his German shepherd to help sniff out concealed enemy positions and help keep us from walking into an ambush We also had two Kit Carson scouts—two Vietnamese soldiers to act as advisors and interpreters, bringing us up to a full strength company including an army intelligence officer. We guessed the Marine Corps had to borrow an intelligence officer from the army because we didn't have any. Someone once said, "The only difference between the Marine Corps and the Boy Scouts was that the Boy Scouts had adult leadership." We thought they might be right.

Religious Services

Before leaving the Rock Pile base, we had one last church service. One chaplain held Catholic, Jewish, and Protestant services for anyone who wanted to attend. The chaplain would preach about loving God and our fellow man, but at the end, he would always say, "Let's go out there a kill a bunch of gooks. We hoped God would understand and have mercy on us for the killing we were doing in the name of freedom. We also hoped he didn't pay any attention to the prayers that the NVA were praying." They were heathen, and we were just sinners. Like there was a difference!

There wasn't much to say about my prayer life in Vietnam. I suppose my thoughts were to use God like a spare tire, instead of a close friend.

> Someone once said, "They who use God for a spare tire need to have more flats."

I had plenty of flats, reasons to pray, but I just didn't unless there was a problem. My dad was the one that kept me covered in prayer, but I didn't really appreciate his prayers as much as I should have even though I was glad he did. Carrying my religious medal around my neck made me feel good, but I really knew it didn't do anything to keep me safe. What really protected me was having someone praying for me who had a personal relationship with Jesus Christ and that was my dad. My father didn't know where I was or what I was doing, but God did. That made all the difference in the world. It seemed like I had a knack for being in the wrong place at the wrong time, or maybe it was the opposite. I was always in the right place at the right time because somehow I was never physically wounded. I did have shrapnel holes in my flak jacket from a Chicom grenade but was untouched by it. I would sometimes wonder why everyone else got wounded or killed, but not me. I had a lot of close calls, but nothing ever stuck. The only thing that I could ever account it to was that God was watching over me because my dad was asking him to.

I don't know if anyone has ever given a good enough answer as to why some live and some die from being involved in catastrophic situations. Most people conclude that it's just their time to go. I don't necessarily agree with that opinion, but I do believe that God sees, hears, and is very aware of our every situation. He can intervene and extend life to even an unbeliever if God's children will only ask him to do so. It is then up to God as to how he intervenes in the person's life. Jesus came to seek and save the lost.

Battlefield Redemption

I heard a story about two marines in Kilo Company. One was a squad leader named Robert, and the other was an eighteen-year-old squad member named Josh. Josh started worrying about dying in the meat grinder of Vietnam and asked his buddies what they knew about God. Robert was the only one that knew much of anything, and he was Roman Catholic. He told Josh that he would have to learn the catechism, repent, and confess his sins to the priest and be baptized. Josh was overwhelmed by the assignment as he realized there was no time to waste in trying to get it all done. His only problem was being afraid he might get killed before he finished doing everything he thought God required of him. In his simplicity, Josh was trying to reach out to God in the only way he knew—without understanding the concept of simple faith in God. He was actually trying to touch God through his simple obedience and didn't know it, but God did.

A month later, their platoon got into a firefight; and in the midst of the fighting, Josh was mortally wounded by being shot in the head. He fell backward onto Robert, and in his dying breathe, he asked Robert to baptize him. Robert poured water from his canteen onto Josh's forehead as his eyes rolled back, and he died.

There's More

I've learned throughout my life that God is loving and merciful. I also believe Josh was reaching out to God with everything his faith could do. I also believe that Josh is with that loving God today because he trusted God to forgive him. Many of Josh's family and friends knew nothing of what was happening in his life, but God did. God knew, saw, and understood Josh. He took him at the right time in ensure his future in heaven.

Avoiding Hot Metal and Bullets

I personally didn't want to get a Purple Heart. I just wanted to be a corporal. I couldn't ever figure out why they gave the wounded a medal anyway. Whenever someone got injured, they would take them out of the bush to a piece of civilization called a hospital. There, you got to sleep all day in a soft bed with clean sheets and pillow, hot food, ice-cold water, air-conditioned rooms, television, and pretty nurses. Then they gave you a medal so you could tell everybody how brave you were and how you suffered for your country. If you didn't get wounded, you went nowhere! You stayed in the bush to fight the enemy, leeches, mosquitoes, 118-degree temperature with every stinging, biting critter out in the wilds to eat on you. You got nothing for your efforts and perseverance, and no one ever heard about you. I figured they gave the medal to the wrong guys. They should have given us a medal for not getting wounded. Maybe like a perfect-attendance pin or something like a Red Heart that read, "Thanks for sticking around."

Killing Time

As we continued waiting around to move out, someone in the artillery unit next to where we had gathered pulled out a football and threw it to Bill Bushey. Bushey was a sports nut who couldn't turn down any opportunity to play ball, and he could always get a game started in no time. It didn't matter what kind of ball it was—baseball, soccer, or football. He loved it all. His ambition was to go back to college for two more years and become a high school physical education coach. In a couple minutes, two teams had formed up, and a game was under way. Some marines played while the rest watched and cheered. A few of us in the rear of the column just continued kicking back against our packs and enjoying the power nap we were getting. We knew that once we got up and put on our eighty pounds of gear, there would be no resting until we had reached our objective for that day.

We were aware of several command changes in the past few days as we found out that Captain Goodwin had turned the company over to First Lieutenant Richmond O'Neill. Goodwin and Ollie North would be heading back to the battalion rear area for the remainder of their tours. We were also losing Rudisell and a couple other old salts that had been with us for a long time. O'Neill was a capable, seasoned officer, but it just seemed like a bad time to be losing so many good marines at the beginning of an important operation along the DMZ. It was always a good idea to be at your best when heading into an area like Mutter's Ridge, but it just happened to be their time to rotate out of the bush, whether we needed them or not. Regardless of the loss in experience, we'd have to continue on and make do without them. We just hoped all the new grunts were quick learners because our lives could depend on it.

We began to hear the order being passed for everyone to fall in. The football game ended, and the ball was returned to its owner. Everyone began grabbing their own gear and helping each other to stand up, getting the heavy packs situated and strapped down. We dressed as always so we could drop our packs and join the battle in one quick motion, knowing that once a battle started, there would not be a minute to lose.

The POGs standing around the artillery gun pits watching us get ready to leave had a gloom-and-doom expression on their faces. They knew we were going out into the belly of the beast, and some of us would probably not be coming back alive. It was obvious by their demeanor that they were glad they weren't going with us. We tried to look brave and unshaken, but we couldn't help but wonder who would not be coming back with us. I felt sick in my stomach at the thought of what we were about to face in the days to come. Even the bravest among us were possibly having second thoughts about leaving this secure base but would never have admitted it. They were trapped and entangled by their own pride and fearless comments to their subordinates.

It was amazing to watch how we transformed from a friendly football game to a skilled killing machine that was all about business and had very little compassion on their enemy. We would take care of those who needed help, like women and children, but if they had an enemy uniform on or they were NVA sympathizers, they would be shot on sight.

I have known many so-called tough guys in my life, but most of them were a bunch of wannabes. These young marines were the real deal that fought to the death time after time. We were seasoned combat veterans who were as committed to killing our enemy as he was to killing us. There was no other way to be if you wanted to keep on living, and we did.

As we began filing out of the compound, we stretched into a long column of 203 men. We kept about twenty feet between each man as we silently melted into the bush once again. Soon the Rock Pile base was out of sight, and Mutter's Ridge was looming in the distance about five miles away. It would take about a week of slowly patrolling the terrain, searching for the elusive enemy until we finally reached our final destination.

Arriving At The Ridgeline

During the nine days prior to reaching the ridgeline, we only had sporadic contact with the NVA. There were plenty of signs of their presence, so we had to always stay alert to the danger that surrounded us. We knew that eventually we would run into each other, and our only hope was that we would see them before they spotted us. Our adrenaline constantly pumped as we were living in hostile territory and going from one firefight to another as our brain referenced and filed each event for future flashbacks into our upcoming never-ending war.

Early on the morning of September 12, we were beginning to start our final patrol around the base of the ridgeline before ascending up the side the next day. We could see Lima Company in the distance moving down the top of the ridgeline ahead of us. They were lining up their men to move out when suddenly, we heard a large explosion. Their point man had just started to lead out their column when they were hit from the front with a claymore directional mine. A firefight quickly erupted, lasting only a few minutes before the NVA ran back into the bush. Lima Company ended up with one dead and several wounded. A few minutes later, the medevac choppers flew in to pick up the casualties. It was starting out to be just another day on Mutter's Ridge, and tomorrow, it would be our turn. Our BNGs were becoming intensely hypersensitive as they were quickly learning that complacency was not an option around this area of the DMZ. An attack like that not only killed and maimed those directly in the ambush, but it affected everyone as it put us all on high alert and wondering who would be next. Those who were here to get action and medals were asking themselves, "Is this what I really want?" It was too late now because we were here in the tiger's home territory. We had just been put on notice, and we would have to start stalking the tiger in a more determined way.

In times like this, you can be terrorized by the possibility of thinking they were the attackers, or you could take the initiative and attack them. If you let fear stop you, you'll die. According to some NVA prisoners, the US Marines were some of the fiercest fighters they had ever come up against. The marines always kept coming no matter what. We had learned from the marines that served in wars before us that you have to take the fight to the enemy. It's more dangerous if you don't. The Marines of WWI were called devil dogs because the Germans thought they were hounds from hell. They kept charging the enemy positions like there was no other option but get to the enemy and kill him.

In WWII, the marines that stormed the shores of the Pacific Islands did not want to die, but they knew they had to get out of the landing crafts and get off the beach to kill the enemy. They had no other choice but to fight because the Japanese would not hesitate to torture and kill those who surrender. Their religion and philosophy taught them to never give up, and if someone did, they forfeited their right to live. In Korea, it was the same thing. Even though they were half frozen and starved, they had to keep fighting. The North Koreans and Chinese had no mercy on those who gave up. If the Americans kept on fighting and killed enough of the enemy, who knows? They might even get to live a long life.

Mutter's Ridge

As we stood looking at the ridgeline for the third time in 1969, we felt somewhat like those former marines who'd gone before us. We understood the consequences of not taking the fight to the enemy. We couldn't run or walk away from our mission, and it would probably come to a major fight before it was over. We just had to remember who we were and why we were here. We were United States Marines!

The NVA also knew we were not alone. We had elements of support such as artillery, air superiority, including the AC47 gunship called Puff the Magic Dragon and Big Mo, the battleship *Missouri*, steaming just off the coast within range if we needed them. With all our support on hand, the NVA usually chose to fight at night or catch us in an ambush and then disappear back into the jungle. They fought like a tiger, stalking their prey and attacking when you were most vulnerable. We tried to limit our vulnerability to zero percent, but it was not always easy to do.

The enemy also knew the marines were disciplined and aggressive warriors. Their fire team leaders were trained to organize a four-man team to attack the enemy or call in artillery. It was like fighting an army of four-man teams that could operate together or independently of each other. Anytime the enemy stayed around to fight, the marines would come out on top.

On the evening of September 12, a squad leaders' meeting was called to get the details for going up the side of the ridge the next morning. Lieutenant Bowen told us that our platoon would be taking the point position for the company, and I needed to pick out who would be walking point for our platoon. The point man needed to know where to start from and the several points to stop along the way until we reached the top of the ridge. Because the danger level in this area was so high, we would leave early enough so we wouldn't have to rush getting to the top. We really appreciated that. I returned back to my squad with the news and the assignment of walking point for the next day. They were not thrilled to say the least about leading the company up the hillside on the first day. I let them groan and moan for a few minutes and then told them to shut up because we were going to do this thing. Everyone began laughing as we expelled some of our tension and settled down to talk. Every man in our squad was capable of walking point, and they had taken their turn at one time or another. Some were better and more experienced than others, and there were a lot of them to choose from, but who would I pick to lead us into the unknown?

I once again began thinking about my being more scared than anyone else and me telling them to do what I was too scared to do myself. I hated those words. The thought kept coming back to me. Would I be able to live with myself for making such a selfish decision? After carefully considering my options, I reluctantly decided to take point myself. The others had always taken the job in the past without complaint, but now it was my turn. After all, the last time we were in this area, I was out sick with malaria for part of the operation and had missed the ambush in May 25. After explaining the situation to Lieutenant Bowen, he said that it was up to me. I then confessed to him that for some unknown reason, I'd started having a strange premonition of me getting hit. I'd never experienced anything like this before and didn't know what to do about it. I was told to just relinquish the position and let somebody else get shot at.

My stupid reply was, "Nah, I'll do it. I want to see what's going to happen." Regardless of the unusual, heavy, depressed emotion

I was experiencing, I'd still take point position and be especially vigilant while wondering what was going to happen. *Dumb!*

> A study once showed that those who have the greatest amount of guts have the least amount of brains. It's a trade off of sorts.

Apparently, that's me. I used to joke that I had already killed the NVA soldier that was supposed to kill me. This could be the time we'd find out for sure. Regardless, I'd made my decision, and now I'd stick with it and find out how it would all turn out. It had to be one of the dumbest things I've ever done.

The Ridgeline

Our morning started out around 07:00 as our column formed up and started to move out. The temperature and humidity began to rise quickly as the scorching sun was already beating down on us. As we moved through the elephant grass and on to the incline leading up to the Ridgeline, there were no distinct fragrances of jungle flowers or plant life in the air as everything in the area had been touched, scarred, and burnt by the war. Once we began our trek up the hillside, there was very little shade to block out the sun because the vegetation was dead due to the excessive use of the defoliant called agent orange. We were never informed about the dangers of what they were spraying on us, and we didn't know if it was a bug, mosquito, or weed killer. We were told to ignore it because it was for our good. By noon time, the temperature was well over one hundred degrees, and we were still trying to climb the steep incline that led up to the top of the ridgeline itself. Several of our men collapsed as they became exhausted from the excessive heat. Our corpsmen called for canteens of water to be passed to them so the overheated casualties could be cooled off quickly. Everyone tried to ignore the plea for giving our precious water to some guy in another platoon that we didn't even know.

Someone laughingly mentioned that we could get more marines, but the water was hard to come by. Most of us carried the extra weight of six canteens of water because we had prior experiences of being without the valued liquid. There was no water on Mutter's Ridge, and what they choppered in to us tasted like detergent, making it almost undrinkable. We reluctantly gave up our canteens in hopes of being resupplied later on when we reached the top. The overheated marines had to be carried, and their gear had to be passed out among their squad members as it

★★★ ═══173

became even more laborious to scale the hill before us. Everyone tried to stay hydrated so we could keep moving until we reached the top where we could rest and cool off in a more secured area. Much to our dismay, as we neared the crest of the ridgeline, I came across a human skull with the name Kilo written on it. We could only guess who had placed it there and hoped it was not a sign of things to come. We buried the skull in a shallow grave and kept moving.

Around 14:00, we finally reached the top and saw there were a couple of bomb craters with water in them. The corpsmen laid the overheated marines in the water so they could cool off quickly before being medevaced out. The water was wet and cool but was too nasty and polluted to drink from. This was NVA territory, and it was always a good policy to not drink any water we found. It was better to be safe than sorry. The nasty water was only good for pouring on overheated and delirious marines so we could save and conserve our good stuff for drinking.

One of our overheated medevacs named Private First Class Drager was always talking about him being an atheist like it meant he was a tough guy or something. We noticed in his moment of delirium, he kept hollering out something about "God help me! God help me!" It's amazing how things change, and you get real religious when you think you might be dying. We thought it was funny.

They never told us much about the agent orange they were using to kill the vegetation. We thought it was a great idea, but the problem was they were spraying it on us too. We lay on the ground at night and unknowingly rolled around in the stuff. We got our water wherever we could find it, and it was full of agent orange. We must have been really naive because it was everywhere, and we saw no danger to us.

About thirty minutes after we got to the top, the choppers finally arrived to pick up the medevacs and drop off some water for us. Lieutenant North came out on one of the choppers with a cold beer for each of us. Some general had sent it out to us as a token of his appreciation. An army officer came out to join up with Kilo Company just long enough to coordinate with an army DC-3 airplane that was equipped with loud speakers. The aircraft was flying over the DMZ, telling the NVA to give up and they would be taken care of. It was like the marines are here to take you prisoner, so you might as well give up. We knew the gooks would either give up or get mad, and they would let us know their decision in the coming days. The message was humiliating to a formidable army like the NVA, just as it would have been to us. The DC-3 attempted to convince them to give up backfired on us and just made them mad. The grunts couldn't believe their leaders had the audacity to try such a stupid move on the NVA. What were they thinking?

By the time our supplies arrived and our medevacs taken out, it was 15:30. It was getting late in the afternoon when they told me to head down the trail that ran on the top of the ridgeline.

Normally, we avoided walking on trails, but we had to make up for lost time, and that was the quickest way to get to where we would hold up for the night. They told me to just stay vigilant and keep walking. They would pass the word up to let me know when to stop. Walking trails, especially up there, was an open invitation to get ambushed and my premonition of getting hit was still heavy on my mind as we made our way down the path.

L/Cpl. Mike Mucyn was behind me as my shadow man, and L/Cpl. Eddie Cavazos was following behind him. The three of us were walking point together as they were backing me up. Cavazos didn't have to be so close to the front of the column because he was within days of rotating home, but he chose to because of his experience in the bush. None of these guys ever backed down when they were needed, and up here, we had to be at our best.

About an hour later, I walked up on a brand-new .45 caliber pistol lying on a piece of plastic. It was nickel plated and looked immaculate. I immediately dropped my pack and untied my rope so I could lasso it like a cowboy in case it was a booby trap. As I was making my lasso, Cavazos walked up to the pistol and picked it up before he could be stopped. He said with his heavy Spanish accent, "Look what I found!" I stood there with my rope in hand, looking like I'd either found a rope or lost my horse. I just shook my head at what could have been a bad situation and told him to be a little more careful picking up nice weapons lying on a trail. They might be booby-trapped the next time. Because Cavazos didn't get killed picking up the pistol and being he was scheduled to go home in a few days, I congratulated him on his find. Apparently, we had walked up on some NVA officer cleaning his pistol. He took off running while leaving his weapon behind. He must have really hated that.

I tied my rope back on my pack and again started walking down the trail.

Cavazos told me years later that an officer had confiscated his pistol as he was checking out in Da Nang to rotate home.

Ambush

About a half hour later, around 17:00, the word was passed up for me to hold up. We would stay on the hill I'd just crossed over for the night. Most hilltops along the ridge had fighting holes that had already been dug on previous operations. This place was one continuous battlefield.

The three of us in the front of the column continued walking down the trail to about fifteen feet from the edge of the perimeter. We set up security, watching the trail that was leading down the ridgeline while everyone else started cleaning out their fighting hole. Mucyn and Cavazos came up on my right side while constantly watching down the trail for intruders. We all got ready to sit down and then...

As I began to lean backward, letting my eighty-pound pack pull me to the ground, Cavazos shouted out, "*Gooks!*" He and Mucyn started firing their weapons to our front while they were running back up the hill to get out of the kill zone. In that instant, I was caught off balance from my pack pulling me down, so I couldn't do anything but fall to the ground. There was no chance for me to run and get out from the ambush site. I was caught out in the open and within fifteen feet from the ambush position. Everything started to appear like it was moving in slow motion. My eyes began scanning the bushes in front of me only to see five NVA soldiers squatting down in the bushes with their rifles pointed directly at me. The one on the end nearest me had his AK47 rifle aimed right at my head. His buddy sitting next to him said something, and the guy opened fire on me with full automatic. The heat and the blast from the rifle hit me in my face, knocking me backward and landing on top of my pack. There was nothing that could be done for me. He had surely hit me in the forehead, and I was dying. The ambush team could see my every move, and if they didn't think I was dying or dead, they would shoot me again. My only thought was to not look at them and make them think I was dead.

Rolling out of my pack and over onto my stomach so they couldn't see my face, I made my body go limp. If he saw me breathing, he would shoot me a second time. I lay there, waiting for the bullets to come ripping through my body. My left hand was nearest the ambush area and could be seen, so I made it start convulsing in a death-like dance. I'd seen other men die and how their body reacted in death, and these guys needed to know it was over for me. My buddies began returning fire, and the NVA became occupied with them rather than me. I tried to breathe as little as possible, hoping my rigid flak jacket would conceal any movement my breathing would cause. Apparently, it worked. The ambush was only fifteen feet away, and we had stopped just short of the kill zone. There was a firefight going on over top of me between the marines and the NVA, and all I could do was play dead. With my right hand, I touched my forehead, and there was no blood. He had missed me completely. This must have been my premonition of dying. Only God had intervened in my behalf.

It would be years later before I'd find out the full story of God's intervention and how he used my dad in praying for my protection that day.

While playing dead in the first few minutes of the ambush, my initial thoughts were, "God help me, please. Don't let me die here." Then my thoughts turned to my father, and I began thinking like a little child again. I thought, *If my daddy was here, he would come over, pick me up, and carry me to safety.* It was strange for me to think of my dad in such a childish way. I couldn't remember ever calling him daddy. What had caused me to think of my dad in such an unusual way? I found out why. A friend and former helicopter pilot told me years later that when they would listen to the black boxes recovered in air crashes, the entire crew could be heard crying for either their mommies, daddies, or Jesus as they were going to their death. They became childlike and cried out for the one they had the most confidence in. That's what was happening to me. My dad was ten thousand miles away, and he didn't have any idea of what was happening to me right then, but God did. He delivered me because somebody was praying for me.

About twenty minutes later, the fighting was over, and the enemy soldiers had broken off contact and were vanishing back into the bush. The marines came down to where I was and helped me up. They were all surprised to see me alive and not bleeding all over the place. My helmet had not been quite as fortunate. It had a bullet hole in the front and out the back along with one hitting and ricocheting off the top. I immediately went up the hill to the first fighting hole I came to and sat down with Renfro and Ham as I tried to calm my nerves down. The only thing I said was, "Man, they were trying to kill me!" They laughed and agreed.

Everyone that knew about my premonition of dying just looked at me and shook their head in amazement. My thoughts of dying quickly vanished, and the unnerving feeling never came back again. It would also be the last time for me walking point. Someone else could do it from now on, regardless of what my dad had told me.

From our late-afternoon contact, we knew the NVA had located us and their deadly aerial assault would be starting soon. All we could do in the time being was dig in a good defensive perimeter and wait for the mortar and possible ground attack to begin. This day would definitely be part of my never-ending war.

A Shot in the Dark

After the late afternoon ambush on September 13, we knew the NVA had located our position and the fire works would be starting soon. All we could do was dig in a good defensive perimeter and wait to see what they were going to do that night. We had lost one of our corpsmen in the firefight that had followed the ambush. I felt bad about not detecting the ambush site ahead of us, and if we hadn't got the word to hold it up, I would have walked even closer to them than what we had. It was just a miracle that we didn't lose even more men that day. Thank the Lord!

About sunset, the aerial attack started; and for the next two hours, we endured a constant barrage of incoming mortars. We took several casualties including our Platoon Sergeant Wetterstrom. He and Lieutenant Bowen were checking on our fighting holes when he got caught out in the open and was blown off the ridge by an incoming mortar. Several marines had to go down the side and bring him back up for medevac. Cpl. Dan Salles became our platoon sergeant from then on.

As the darkness fell on the jungle, the long night of waiting for the enemy to attack was upon us. The first assault of a mortar barrage was over. Now we just had to wait for it to be followed up by an all-out attack by heavily armed and motivated ground troops trying to breech our lines. The hours of waiting for a nighttime battle to commence has got to be the most gut-wrenching times ever. Death seems to be in the air as the Grim Reaper stands by waiting to claim the fallen. The jungle is home to the enemy, and by dusk, he has left his hiding place to stalk his prey. He moves like a hungry tiger, searching for the least suspecting victims until he pounces, ripping the life right out of them.

Crouching low in our fighting holes, we wait for the adversary to come and find us to their own demise. We are prepared to meet and destroy him on his own ground. There will be no smoking or sleeping tonight until the battle is over and the enemy is dead; then, we can rest again. Tonight, along with the cloud cover that has blocked out any light from the moon, the heavy triple canopy jungle vegetation has caused it to become pitch dark, cutting our visibility to near zero. Everyone is straining their eyes as we try to see anything moving out in front of us. We'll first use our claymore infantry mines and grenades against the approaching enemy instead of our rifles so as not to give our position away. Once we open up with our small arms fire, it will be an all-out attack, including hand-to-hand combat. They will, by that time, know exactly where our fighting holes are located by the rifle fire illuminating our positions. Sitting in the darkness, our gut feeling tells us that the NVA are close by and getting ready to attack. We can hear noises in the jungle that sound like someone moving through the dense vegetation, but we could not see anyone The suspense is growing by the minute. Within the past hour or so, we had come to a place in our lives where nothing mattered at this moment except staying alive and killing our adversary. Our future, our possessions, and our relationships, present and future, didn't matter at all right now and wasn't even on our minds because everything we had and wanted was depending on the outcome of this night. It came down to who would live and who would die. We were fighting for our right to live, and we just wanted to get it on and get it over with. *Oorah!*

Sometime during the night, we began to hear the familiar sound of a low flying aircraft circling the ridge. He was humorously called Puff the Magic Dragon. It was an air force AC47 cargo plane, carrying three mini-Gatling guns that fired three thousand rounds per minute each. They could cover a football field with one passover, placing a bullet in every square foot of the field. Every fifth round they fired was a phosphorus-tipped tracer that ignited en route to its target, showing the gunners where the bullets were hitting. It looked like a perforated line of red-tipped bullets coming out of the aircraft and heading toward its target. It was an awesome sight to see unless he was shooting at you.

About an hour or so later, as Puff was making his third pass over the area we were encamped in, the moon popped out of the clouds and exposed the gunship flying about two thousand feet above us. Suddenly, a single rifle shot rang out, splitting the silence. It sounded like it was only a short distance from our company's position deep in the jungle. Pfcs Renfro, Ham, and I whispered jokingly about the possibility of a large number of NVA quietly moving through the bush, setting up to attack us when this idiot, Bubba, decided to impress his buddies by shooting down this American airplane. We could imagine his comrades grabbing hold of him and roughly asking why did he do that? It was too late for them. Puff instantly responded back by firing two of his Gatling guns into the area from where the rifle shot had come from. The imposing army never had time to run as they died where they stood. It was a massacre. Later in life, I would hear of a rednecks famous last words: "Watch this, man." I'd always think of Bubba.

We quietly cheered for Puff as it rained death from above onto the NVA Army. A lot of our attackers had died in a matter of minutes, and we didn't have to fire a shot. We'll never know what the rifle shot was really about or how things would have turned out if Puff hadn't showed up. We only knew the mysterious shooter had given his unit's position away and the results that followed.

The jungle was quiet for the rest of the night, and the NVA suspended their activity to keep from taking more losses. We all quietly agreed that God had used Puff to stop a nighttime battle before it ever got started. I'd write my dad and tell him about the incident and ask him to keep praying for us as we were definitely in the belly of the beast. We were also one day closer to getting off this death trap called Mutter's Ridge.

The Patrol Continues

Throughout the morning of the fourteenth, we slowly and methodically worked our way up to a small hill that was in the shadow of our final destination—Hill 410. This hill before us was the largest and highest hill on the ridgeline, and it was the most notorious for large firefights. A battalion of NVA could easily camouflage themselves out of sight in its dense jungle-like terrain and bunker-type emplacements that were there from earlier battles. There was obviously a large number of NVA still on Hill 410 because when our fighter aircraft would drop their bombs, a heavy amount of enemy small arms would return fire on them as they pulled up from their bomb run. According to the grapevine, our battalion thought they would have been gone by now, but apparently, they hadn't got the word that the marines were here, and they were supposed to leave. As the day progressed, the small arms fire never seemed to diminish even though the bombs kept dropping. We began to wonder what kind of resistance we were going to face tomorrow morning as we assaulted an occupied and heavily fortified hill.

The planners of Operation Idaho Canyon anticipated the NVA would move off the hill just before the marine ground troops got there. According to the information we received, contact was expected to be at a minimum. We were assured that with all our support units assisting us, the enemy really didn't want a head on confrontation. The NVA would usually move at night when they could leave undetected in the darkness and avoid a major fight. The planners assumed the enemy units would be inside the DMZ by the time we arrived. The grunts knew the first rule on Mutters' Ridge was you never assume anything. We began to notice the enemy machine gunners had stopped firing at the attacking fighter jets later that afternoon. We didn't know if they had hunkered down in their bunkers or moved off the hill to fight another day. We wouldn't know until we went over there to look for ourselves. Just before dark, our platoon was sent back out into the bush to set up ambushes again. One thing we couldn't help but notice was the moonlight was so bright we could have easily read a newspaper without any assisting light source. A major blunder: battalion headquarters must not have realized the problem of it being a full moon that week, and the enemy did not have any darkness in which to move their units in. They did the only other logical thing they could do. They hunkered down and waited for us to come to them.

Throughout the night, Puff was scouring the ridgeline looking for any enemy movement below. He would have ripped them apart if they had tried to leave. The gunship did not even need flares to see the enemy troops as he unknowingly blocked the NVA retreat from the ridgeline. We had zero contact throughout the night because no one was moving around in the moon light. After sunrise, we packed up our gear and returned back to our company perimeter hoping for an easier day in patrols because of our being tasked with pulling ambushes the night before.

September 15, 1969. As soon as our squads returned back to our company perimeter, we were told to hurry up and eat our C rations breakfast. First platoon was going to pull a search-and-destroy mission on Hill 410. Lieutenant Bowen was the senior platoon commander with Kilo Company, and it was his call as to who would get the mission that day. The probability of us making contact with at least a small number of NVA was very high and all the officers wanted to be part of that. There was a chance to get some combat experience of taking a hill on the infamous Mutter's Ridge, and any officer in their right mind would have jumped at the chance. It was a once in a lifetime opportunity. The enlisted peons had no opinion or say so concerning the situation, but we were already worn out from our ambush duty the night before. Now we'd have to spend the day hunting down any stragglers that were left behind to hold the hill. We didn't think there would be too many defenders still there, but we knew it didn't take but one with an automatic rifle to do a lot of damage. There was no way of telling how many NVA were over there, but we knew it was going to be a long day for first platoon.

Today would be the defining moment for Kilo Company in this operation as Hill 410 was known for major battles in the past. If there was going to be a head-to-head fight with the NVA, this would be the day for it. This was their homeland, and the NVA had fought many battles on this hill before. They were familiar with every inch of this mountain. On the other hand, this would be the third time for our most seasoned veterans to be here and first time for many of our men in Kilo Company. In our simplistic way of thinking, we figured that Operation Idaho Canyon would soon be over, and if we could just get past today, the rest would be gravy. We just wanted to get away from Mutter's Ridge in one piece.

Getting Ready to Go

As we were eating our C ration breakfast, artillery shells from the Rock Pile began slamming into the hill in front of us as they began softening up the target area before we went over. We thought they must have been short on ammunition because it only lasted for about thirty minutes. It was like knocking on someone's door before you kick it in. Cpl. Bill Bushey came over to where our squad was sitting and sat down with us. He wanted to make sure he saw everyone before being rotated home along with seeing my famous helmet with the bullet holes in it. Bill only had three days before being rotated out of the bush to return home. We talked and laughed about what had been going on for the past week and what was anticipated for that day. In the early morning squad leaders' meeting, Bushey's squad had been given the assignment of taking point. Pfc. Donald Liebl would be walking the front position because he was Bushey's best point man. With the summit of Hill 410 being about one thousand yards from the adjacent hill we were on, we knew it could be a short or a very long trip for us to the top depending on how much opposition we ran into. Our orders were to exit the hill as soon as we made contact. They'd let our elements of support destroy the hill for us.

As we finished eating, we started getting our gear on to leave for the patrol. We all thought a lot of Bill and told him to be safe. He had trained me to be a squad leader, and he was the kind of guy everyone liked. Everybody, including me, thought they were Bushey's best friend. As he started to walk away, I told him to keep his eyes open and to be careful up there. He grinned and said, "I'll see you guys at the top of the hill." We nodded so long, and he took off to join his squad. We knew there was going to be a fight that day, but we had no idea that this mission would change the lives of Kilo Company Marines forever. Today would be a watershed moment and one of the culminating factors in our never-ending war.

At 08:00, the platoon lined up in a long column. Bushey's second squad led off with Honsa's first squad following in behind. Lieutenant Bowen's command post fell in line along with the extras and my third squad coming up last. One of the extras we had with us was a dog handler with his German shepherd. It was previously decided that we would not need him until we reached the bunker complex at the top of the hill. This was something that was done quite often when using a dog, but today, we would end up wishing we'd put him up in the front of the column. He might have smelled trouble along the way and warned us of the impending danger. Hindsight is always 20/20.

Private First Class Liebl was told to take the trail up the hill so we could hurry and get to the top. It was never a good idea to hurry or use trails on Hill 410, but it's one of the things you learn through experience on Mutter's Ridge if you lived long enough. Our CO, First Lt. Richmond O'Neill, was our only Mutter's Ridge veteran officer, and he was not with us on this patrol. He watched our platoon leaving from the command hill and disappearing into the jungle. Our order to get off the hill as soon as we made contact was different from anything we'd ever done before. Artillery, gun ships, and air wing was waiting for us to exit the hill so they could level it. This new simple plan of action sounded good, but we'd never tried this tactic before. We had always pushed forward to engage and assault the enemy to defeat them. This time would be different.

Private First Class Liebl led the column down the trail and up the narrow finger, a natural bridge, that would lead to the top of the hill. If we hurried and passed a certain point in the jungle growth, we could spread out in the open and cover more ground. The jungle we were passing through had a drop off on one side that went down forty to fifty feet. It was starting to look like ambush alley to us, but all we could do was stay hypervigilant to our surroundings as the column continued to move forward.

Bushey had taken up a position near the front of his squad. It was a dangerous place to be, but he was experienced and knew his knowledge and leadership could be better used near the front. He didn't want to be a hero; he just wanted to be at the best possible position to lead and take care of his men.

As the platoon moved through an area of triple canopy, the jungle began to close in around us. As it did, we began to lose visual contact with our company that was located on the hill behind us. Our column was spread out for about fifty yards as my third squad began entering into the jungle area. Suddenly, the column stopped. Everyone dropped down on one knee to wait out the delay of what was holding us up. It became deathly silent as we became aware that something was not right. The only sounds we could hear was everyone's rifle safety flipping to full automatic. Liebl had moved up the trail without seeing anything suspicious until he'd unknowingly passed through the large ambush area. He then detected a claymore mine hanging in one of the trees on the left side of the trail only yards from him. He dropped down on one knee as he stopped the column from moving forward and started warning them with hand signals of a possible ambush coming from both sides of the trail. Bushey went forward and approached Liebl to find out what was going on. They both suddenly realized they were inside of an ambush kill zone, and they had to do something quickly. Bushey started to go back down the trail to warn his squad of the impending danger as they would all drop to the ground to avoid the hail storm of shrapnel and bullets and begin firing on the enemy positions to the right.

A reinforced NVA platoon was lying in wait and had allowed two-thirds of the marine platoon to enter the ambush area. The enemy ambush team saw they were losing their chance of surprise and decided to launch the attack by exploding a series of claymore mines that had been placed just inside the tree line to the left and lined the trail.

Boom! Boom! Boom! Claymore mines exploded throwing glass, nails, and sharp pieces of metal at the marines as simultaneous small- and medium-sized weapons erupted from seemingly everywhere. First platoon had been caught in a deadly platoon-sized ambush where they would sustain many casualties before the day was over. The battle had just begun.

The Perfect Ambush

Cpl. William Bushey and Pfc. Jerry Gatlin were killed in the opening volley of the ambush. Before the marines could respond, the entire enemy ambush site exploded in flying shrapnel and bullets. The NVA had laid out a horseshoe-shaped ambush with machine guns facing the marines from the front and soldiers spread out along the right side of the trail. Claymore mines were set up in trees on the opposite side of the trail pointing toward the unsuspecting marines. The ambush team had dug trenches along the right side of the tree line to lay in so they would not be hit by their own shrapnel. They fired their automatic weapons low to the ground, striking their targets about knee high. The projectiles would drop anyone standing, and once they fell, the wounded could either be killed or allowed to live so a corpsman or fellow marine would crawl to get him, providing another target.

We were also caught in a perfect ambush site where we could not be seen by our elements of support. It was in thick jungle vegetation with high hanging leaves that created a triple canopy ceiling above us. With all the air cover we had in our support, they could not fire their weapons because they couldn't see us. We were on our own, and we would have to fight our way out of this mess.

Ambush!

The instant the ambush was sprung; my squad dropped their packs and started moving forward to where the fighting was taking place. We didn't have time to be scared, knowing we had to return fire and attack the ambush area without delay. Our buddies were depending on us to help get them out of the kill zone. The situation was dire from the beginning because there were so few wounded marines up front still able to put up a good defense. They were scrambling to regain a degree of control on the situation although the initial attack had killed or injured most of the platoon.

Lieutenant Bowen had been wounded by shrapnel and small arms fire at the initial execution of the ambush. After the first few minutes of him fighting mental and physical shock, he regained control of himself and began shouting commands to his men. He first thought everyone in the platoon was returning fire to the enemy, but he soon realized they were all dead or wounded. He yelled to move up, but there was no one there to move up. He then began to realize how critical the situation had become. The lieutenant crawled to a log that was lying across the trail and got temporary relief from the grenades that kept landing near him. The entire platoon was under heavy attack as Lieutenant Bowen called for a replacement of his command realizing he was gravely injured. He had been wounded in eight places throughout the right side of his body and was starting to lose consciousness. Lieutenant Peterson's third platoon was then summoned to come over and reinforce first platoon in order to get our men off the hill. About halfway up the trail between the two hills, they were also ambushed by small arms fire and mortars. The enemy knew if they let up their attack on us, we would regain momentum and bring the fight back to them. They kept the assault coming at us as hard and fierce with no letup in sight. Some confusion began to break out among first platoon marines because of the original plan of pulling back at initial contact. Some men were trying to get off the hill as ordered, and others were trying to move up the trail to retrieve the dead and wounded from out of the kill zone. It was naturally assumed that if everything went as planned, we would all get off the hill immediately after contact was made, but that was now impossible. With so few marines remaining uninjured around the ambush site, it was hard to assess the situation and get a plan of action going. The dead and wounded were lying everywhere, and we didn't yet know if everyone in our platoon was accounted for.

As my squad was moving forward up to the ambush site, I picked up a can of M60 machine gun ammunition that was lying abandoned on the trail. I figured by the way things were already going, we might need it before the day was over. As we continued running forward, the injured were passing us trying to get back to the safety of the company perimeter. This was the most wounded marines we had ever encountered, and it was staggering to all of us.

A short way up the trail, we came across Cpl. Dan Salles who was kneeling down at an intersection of footpaths. He was bleeding from several wounds but continued directing reinforcements toward the ambush area. I asked him which way we needed to go. He pointed down one trail and then told me that our point man, Donald Liebl, was down and he was on the other side of the ambush. We had to find and get him out of the kill zone before they finished him off.

The men up front also needed the can of gun ammo I'd picked up along the way. I inwardly groaned at the possibilities of going into the deadly ambush area but knew I'd have to do it. We had to hurry and stop the enemy before they completely wiped us out. My mind was spinning from the melee going on all around us. As we were kneeling down and talking out a strategy, several marines ran up to us. We told them to get up the hill. They replied back to us that the company gunny had just ordered them to get everyone off the hill, ASAP, The two different commands were causing confusion among the troops, and everyone was arguing as of what to do. One of the wounded marines exiting the hill was L/Cpl. Mike Mucyn. He was on his way to the adjoining hill when he stopped to ask me if I thought his wounds were bad enough to get him sent back home. Two large bullet holes were visible in his upper right arm. I told him it looked good enough to me. We laughed and he took off again down the hill. It would be the last time I would see him for another forty years. As far as the marines pinned down by enemy fire was concerned, there was only one thing to do—return fire to get our dead and wounded off the hill and then pull back so the air wing could take over. We couldn't leave until all our men were accounted for. We watched more casualties running past us, bleeding and helping carry each other out of the kill zone. Salles looked at me and pointed. He again said, "They need that gun ammo up there." Again I groaned, fighting the thought of not going further into the kill zone, but then my training took over, and I took off running up the incline. They needed the ammo, and I was carrying it.

Into the Fire

After running up the hill about twenty yards, I came up on Private First Class Alverez who had picked up an abandoned M60 machine gun with another M60 lying on the ground next to it. My first thought was where were the gun teams. Knowing them personally and being with them all the time in the bush, it was inconceivable to think they would ever abandon their weapons unless they were dead or seriously injured. I hoped my friends on the gun teams were not dead, but there was no time to even think about it right now. There were also a lot of rifles lying around the area, and it was not because their owners had thrown them down in the heat of battle and ran away. It was because so many of them had to be carried away. It was mind-boggling from the high casualty count of my friends who were like family to me. By the amount of discarded weapons lying around, there had to be a lot of dead marines. This was my family, and they were being slaughtered in front of me.

As we knelt down along the trail to stay low, Cpl. John Nelson came running up to us as Alverez was loading his M60 machine gun. Alverez told one of us to pick up the other abandoned machine gun lying off to itself. I handed my rifle to Nelson and picked up the machine gun. I had only fired an M60 one other time, and that was in basic training. It was one of those times in life where you just do, without questioning, what has to be done and live with the results. My main reason for me picking up the M60 was that it had a lot more fire power than my rifle did. Under the circumstances, it seemed like the smartest thing to do.

I couldn't escape the questions that kept running through my mind: What happened to the gunners? Where were Torboli, Harper, Richardson, Thompson, and so many other gunners? Every time someone called out, "Guns up," they would come running. Now, they were all gone.

I opened the magazine cover and inserted the first bullet of a fifty-round assault belt. I closed the cover, pulled back the bolt, and fired a couple rounds into the ambush area to make sure the gun worked. The two of us then stood up in a crouching position and started walking forward, blasting everything in our path. We fired both M60s as hard as we could, hoping that even if we didn't kill any enemy soldiers, they would at least think we were counterattacking and pull back their troops. We were making a lot of noise with the weapons firing, and some later said it sounded like a chainsaw running wide open. Several of the marines that had exited off the hill heard all the shooting and came back to help us assault the ambush site. Pfc. Robert DeRusso was one of them. He had just turned eighteen years old a few weeks earlier while in Vietnam.

Misfire!

As we were busy attacking the ambush area, suddenly at the same instant, Alverez ran out of ammunition, and my gun jammed up, bringing our machine gun assault to an abrupt halt. We looked at each other and then dove to the ground as several Chinese Communist grenades came flying at us from the bushes to the right of us. All we could do was ball up into a fetal position and hope we would not get hit. It was hard to get inside of our helmet, but we tried. The grenades went off seconds later, and amazingly, they only hit us with concussion. The shrapnel had blown out between us. They had shaken us up pretty good but drew no blood. Our mini assault had ended, and we started returning fire with the weapons we found lying on the ground around us.

Inside the Ambush Area

Although wounded, Lance Corporal Honso was the only living marine up at the front of the ambush area, and he had only a few rounds left in his M16 rifle when we got to him. He looked flushed and was in shock from being caught in the whirlwind of the ambush and ensuing firefight. There were several dead marines lying around him in the open as everyone else had been carried away to the hill behind us. Honsa said in a low, monotone voice, "There's only one more left" as he motioned with his head further down the trail.

The enemy small arms fire was still relentlessly coming in as we were trying to figure out a plan of what we were going to do. Eight or ten other marines crawled up behind us and started gathering behind the log and back down the trail a few yards.

We told them to stay down low because they were shooting anyone who sat or stood up. The fighting was only about twenty yards apart as both sides were shooting through the bushes as rapidly as they could and throwing grenades at each other. This was amazingly close combat. The fighting was so close to the enemy that if we didn't let our grenade release spoon go before we threw it, the gooks would pick up our grenade and throw them back at us before they exploded.

Life was intense!

Finding Bushey

Someone asked me about the identity of the dead marine that was lying in front of me. I had been using him like a sandbag to shield myself from the grenades and automatic gunfire coming at me from our front. As I paused to look on his dog tag that was laced up in his boot strings, to keep it from rattling, the name read Cpl. William Bushey. I was stunned with a sudden sense of anger and grief as I looked at my dead friend lying there with a pale look of death on his face. I then remembered he only had three days to go before rotating home again. We all hated that he'd dodged death the whole year just to die at the very end. It somehow didn't seem fair, but then again, nothing was fair in this place. Bill didn't really look like himself because he had always been so full of life and laughter, and now he looked almost like a wax manikin, lying motionlessly in front of me. I knew he couldn't hear me, but I still told him I was sorry we hadn't been there for him. That moment in time would be frozen in my memory for the rest of my life, thereby contributing greatly to my own never-ending war. Renfro and Taylor then grabbed him by his shoulders and pulled him away to be carried off in a poncho to the hill behind us. The war was over for him and the others, but there was no time right now to pause and grieve for our friends who were dying all around us. We'd have to wait till later and then spend the rest of our lives doing that. Survivor's guilt would inevitably become a large obstacle for us to process in our upcoming never-ending war.

Help!

Suddenly, we heard Liebl holler, "Help me! Somebody come and get me. I'm hit!" It again registered with all of us that we had to get him out before they finished killing him. Whenever they saw the battle was turning in our favor, they would have no further use of Liebl. They were deliberately keeping him alive in order to kill as many of us as they could. This was a dog fight for Liebl, and we weren't going to let them have him. Marines don't leave marines behind.

As we were returning a heavy volume of small arms fire into the ambush area, we continued moving forward through the kill zone, working our way up to Liebl. One of the M60 gun team from third platoon came crawling up to the log next to me. The assistant gunner named Pfc. Stephen Richardson ended up on my left side and DeRusso on my right. We had told them to stay down due to the low profile incoming fire, but Richardson sat up to throw a grenade, and suddenly—*smack!*—a bullet entered right through his heart. He snatched open his flak jacket, and the blood shot out of his chest in three large spurts. The entry hole in his chest was about the size of a nickel. The bloodstream shot out from him about three feet, then two feet, one foot, and then, he had finished bleeding out. He turned toward me and tried to say something but just mumbled incoherent words. His face was pale with shock and loss of blood as he must have realized he was dying and beyond help. He tried desperately to crawl down the hill but only made it a couple feet before collapsing face-down. I watched him struggle for his last breath, and then he died.

I'd never forget the look of surprise and shock on Stephen's face as he watched in horror his blood gushing out of his chest. He tried to outrun death, but it was too late. A C ration candy bar rolled out of his pant pocket onto the ground. I turned him over and closed his eyes and put the candy bar back into his pocket. Only a few minutes before, that candy bar was his, and he was going to eat it. He was eighteen years old, and he was going to live forever, but that was not to be. I moved aside as a marine behind me pulled him away to be carried over to our company hill. His friend and gun team member Pfc. Lawrence Dutton was firing the machine gun and saw the whole thing. Angered at his friend's death and not thinking, he sat up and started firing his gun wildly into the bushes. He couldn't see the well-camouflaged NVA, but they could see him. The enemy opened fire on him, hitting him five times in the upper chest and neck. He fell backward, then flipped over onto his hands and knees and started crawling toward us saying "I'm hit!" We knew he'd been hit because we could see the bullets striking him and ripping through his flesh and flak jacket.

One of our corpsman HM3 Doc. James Sickles was lying on the ground behind me. He grabbed the gunner and wrestled him over onto his back. He slit a hole in his throat and performed an emergency tracheotomy to keep Dutton from drowning in his own blood. His legs were thrashing about as the doc cut him without any kind of numbing agent. There was no time! Dutton was pulled away from the kill zone and carried to the company hill behind us where other corpsmen could take over, stabilizing him before being medevaced out. I found out through naval medical records thirty years later that due to the corpsman's quick response that day, Dutton lived and returned home to his family.

Meanwhile

As the fighting continued, Liebl kept hollering for us to come and get him. Our forward movement was slow because of the tremendous amount of small arms fire and grenades that were being thrown at us. They were using Liebl to keep us in the kill zone area because they knew that as soon as we pulled back, our air wing would be turned loose on them, bringing an end to the fighting.

One of the problems we had was not knowing the exact spot where Liebl was located. The heavy vegetation and smoke from the battle made it hard to see ahead of us. It hampered the return fire we wanted to produce, but we still continued to advance through the killing field of the ambush toward the downed marine. As we struggled forward, Pfc. Robert DeRusso crawled up behind me. He was a quiet, soft-spoken Hispanic marine that always did his job and never stood out as being a hero type. He grabbed my shoulder to get my attention and said, "Clark, we need to go and get him now!" I told him, "You hold on. We're going to get him out, but you wait for the rest of us!" We didn't need any more dead heroes.

Bob had a strange look on his face as he softly replied, "Someone's got to go get him!" Turning to my left and telling Nelson and the others to move up, I turned back to my right to see that DeRusso had already crawled off without saying a word to anyone. I thought, *Now we have two men to find*. We continued our advancing forward, trying to push the enemy back out of the ambush area so we could get to Liebl. The NVA had our position pinpointed, and we continued taking casualties from mortars, grenades, and small arms fire. At one point in the fighting, several of us had moved out of the triple canopy above us and out into an open area. Lieutenant Peterson passed up a M79 grenade launcher and told me to fire it straight up into the air. They said, "Use it like a mortar." I'd never fired one straight up in the air before mainly because I didn't know where it was going to come down. I wasn't too thrilled about trying it, but they said, "Do it," so I did. We didn't know if it would do any good or not, but we were willing to try anything to break up this stalemate of apposing forces.

Derusso Returns

About thirty minutes later, we heard a familiar voice coming from the thick bushes ahead of us saying, "Don't shoot. It's me!" Bob was slowly dragging Liebl by his collar. He had crawled through the ambush site all alone and found Liebl about forty yards down the trail. Donald had been gutshot about two inches below his navel and had fallen into an anthill. Bob found him covered with ants but was very much alive. No wonder he had been hollering so much for help. He was in utter torment. Doc Sickles started working on Liebl right away as we carried him off the hill to the relative safety of the company area. We were finally able to get everyone off of the hill so the Huey gun ships could take over and destroy the enemy with their rockets and miniguns. Pfc. Snyder and Ritchey covered our withdrawal from Hill 410 as the NVA started mortaring us along the trail. In our rush to get off the hill and avoid getting caught in the bomb run of several attacking jets, we followed everyone leaving Hill 410 and took an alternate trail back to the adjacent hill. We'd mistakenly left our packs on the original trail near the ambush site. No one had picked them up, and they were still lying where we'd dropped them. I asked permission to go back and retrieve the munitions we were carrying inside of them but was denied. Our packs were our home away from home, and losing them was bad. In just a few minutes, we would see our packs being annihilated by a napalm run in an attempt to destroy our ammunition, mines, and mortar rounds we carried inside of them. I also regrettably lost my cigarettes, hot sauce, onions, and five canteens of water I'd been carrying around with me for the entire operation. I really hated that.

The Dying Continues

We would soon be finding out that because the NVA had fought on this hill many times before, they had already preregistered their mortars on our company hill and knew exactly where our fighting holes were positioned. They also knew where our medevac choppers would be coming in to pick up our wounded. They would take pleasure in killing our casualties as they lay out in the open waiting to be choppered out.

The enemy's prior experience on Hill 410 turned out to be a major factor in the events that took place on Mutter's Ridge, September15, 1969.

As we came off Hill 410, we passed several marines wrapped in ponchos. I stopped and told my friend Bushey a final good-bye. The only thing that came to my mind as I looked at him was, "I'm so sorry, Bill. I'm so sorry for your family." He was supposed to be getting married in a week or so, but the wedding flowers would now be for his funeral. Not only had we lost some good marines that day, but we lost some great friends, and our lives would never be the same again.

The first incoming mortar rounds hit in and around our wounded that were waiting for medevac choppers to pick them up. Doc Sickles was still working on Liebl when a mortar round landed next to them and killed them both. The mortar barrage would last for another two hours, causing more casualties. There were so many NVA spread out on the hill that day and so encased in their bunkers that the air raids didn't seem to impede them in their quest to destroy Kilo Company. They continued firing their mortars as our jets were attacking them. We just had to stay in our fighting holes until the barrage let up. We actually hoped they would try to attack us, and we would get another chance to kill some of them, but they didn't. I guess we should be glad they didn't because we were later told that it was estimated to be a battalion of NVA occupying Hill 410 that day.

Medevac Choppers

We couldn't believe the bravery of the medevac choppers as they kept coming in to get our dead and wounded while the mortars continued to fall. The choppers made big targets, and at least one of them crashed on their way back to Vandergrift combat base. The men flying those things had nothing but respect and appreciation from the grunts they were trying to help.

Sometime later that day, after the choppers had departed with all our casualties, and the mortars had gone silent we realized first platoon had been reduced down to six men. Kobra, Nelson, Renfro, DeRusso, Ritchie, and I were the only ones left. Cavazos and Snyder had been flown out of the bush for other reasons. We were dumbfounded, depressed, and shocked. We kept asking each other what happened. We were the good guys, and this kind of thing was not supposed to happen to us. The only bright spot I had that day was when my squad of five marines told me that I was now their platoon commander. Big deal! We all laughed at the thought.

The Final Days

Sometime later in the afternoon of September 15, the word went out "to saddle up." The battle was finally over, and we were moving back down the ridgeline to reassemble our company and receive BNGs to help fill our ranks. Second platoon led off the column as Lieutenant O'Neill's antenna farm and mortars followed in behind. Lieutenant Petersons embattled third platoon filed in next with first platoon, all six of us, bringing up the rear. I could hardly believe what had just happened to the mighty "Killer Kilo." We were the good guys, and this was not supposed to happen to us. We'd always come out on top, or at least, we had before. This time had been different, and our heads were still spinning from the trauma of battle and disbelief of our platoon getting wiped out.

Insult to Injury

As we started to leave the hill, it dawned on me that none of the other platoons had noticed all the weapons lying in a pile off to themselves. They had been brought from Hill 410 earlier in the day and deposited there so they could be choppered out along with our medevacs. They must have been forgotten about, and now it was too late as the choppers had long departed. Someone would now have to carry them, and we were the only ones left on the hill to pick them up.

The other platoons had moved on leaving the six of us behind to shoulder the weapons as best we could. It was like an insult to injury. We had been mostly at fault for destroying the beautiful mountain scenery around us, and now it was up to us to clean up the mess we'd made. As we passed by the cache of weapons, I told everyone to grab up as many as they could possibly carry. We looked like either POGs getting ready to take our group pictures or actors in a cheap comedy war movie that was heading off to war with out arms full of M16 rifles. We were the last six men in our column, and our job was to make sure the NVA weren't following us as we struggled under the weight of the weapons our friends would have normally been carrying. As far as our platoon being tasked with the position of Tail End Charlie, I'm not sure how efficient we were as rear security for our column. We were carrying six rifles each, and we knew if we were attacked, we'd probably get killed while trying to figure out which rifle to shoot.

In a strange twist of fate, it turned out to be a good thing that we'd accidentally left our packs on Hill 410. We couldn't have carried the heavy packs along with the extra load of discarded weapons. Not only were the arms and ammunition heavy, but they were cumbersome as well. The extra burden became a continual, solemn reminder of the day's action as we made our way to our night time bivouac area further down the ridgeline. We were still in contact with the NVA because they had forward observers on adjacent hilltops watching our every move, and before dark, we were mortared twice while moving down the ridgeline. They were also firing a huge 106 recoilless rifle at us from the DMZ. We figured they had probably borrowed from the Rock Pile Artillery Base and Mike Company had lent it to them.

When we finally stopped for the night, I told my squad to take the extra weapons up to the company command area and quietly drop them. Someone else would have to pick them up the next time we moved and carry them the rest of the way. I just knew it wouldn't be us. We were never bothered with them again.

Talking It Out

Just before nightfall, our squad sat down and talked about the events of the day. We talked about how hard it must have been for

Lieutenant O'Neill to watch his new command being torn apart, sitting in a front row seat on the hill next to 410. We considered that on the days prior to the ambush, the NVA realized they could not leave, so they spent their time plotting a battle strategy. They dug their trenches in the best ambush site possible. They set their machine guns up to cover the trail and placed their claymore mines in the trees to do maximum damage to the marines coming up the incline. Not only did they zero in our company's position on the adjacent hill, but the trail between the two hills had been plotted in their sights too. Their mortar teams were on target so they could cut off any reinforcements responding to the platoon caught in the ambush. The NVA were professional soldiers that knew how to engage their enemy.

They had apparently studied the history of previous firefights on Hill 410 and knew exactly where our medevacs would be waiting for the choppers to come in and pick them up. They knew how demeaning and frustrating it would be for us to watch our wounded get slaughtered in front of us while we could do nothing about it. Their plan was to do as much mental and physical damage to Kilo Company before our air wing and artillery was turned lose on them. They had a good plan, and it had worked.

At least twice every day following the ambush, we were hit by artillery from the north. Each time we moved during the next five days, we were slammed again and again. The last time they mortared us was when we were being choppered off the ridge and heading back to Vandergrift Combat Base, bringing an end to Operation Idaho Canyon on September 20, 1969. It was like the NVA were responding to the message we'd given them earlier in the operation of telling them to surrender or else. Our sending a platoon of marines over to engage an NVA Battalion was like carrying a knife to a gunfight. We were simply outgunned and outnumbered. Their message back to us as we were leaving was good-bye and good riddance. The CH46 helicopter my squad boarded in leaving the ridgeline was hit by mortar shrapnel as we were taking off causing the chopper to spit and sputter all the way to Vandergrift. We were sure it would crash before landing, but it didn't. The pilots kept it aloft, and we landed safely.

Idaho Canyon Becomes History

The official "stand down" orders for Operation Idaho Canyon stated that the battalion had met all our operational goals. It also mentioned Kilo Company sustaining quite a few casualties throughout the operation but not the massive amount we remembered. Lieutenant O'Neill told me years later that he remembered our company starting out with 203 men and ending up with 137. That's the way most of us remembered it too.

The Pullout

Idaho Canyon would be the final operation that third battalion, third regiment, third marine division would conduct before being pulled out of Vietnam, as part of then President Nixon's de-Vietnamization program of ending the war. Kilo Company, along with the rest of the battalion, was choppered from Vandergrift to Quang Tri, our battalion headquarters, where the pullout was in full swing. The 3/3/3 had entered the war on May 12, 1965, only expecting to stay there for only thirteen months but got caught up in the deployment of marine units to Vietnam. Third battalion was deployed to Quang Tri province, which was the most northern province of South Vietnam. With the exception of Operation Taylor Common, near An Hoa, the battalion operated in the Northern I Corps area that stretched from Ka Sanh to the demilitarized zone, also known as Leatherneck Square and the meat-grinder. The 3/3 began departing Vietnam on October 7, 1969, and arrived at Camp Pendleton, California the end of 1969. The battalion spent over 1,600 days in Vietnam and conducted forty-eight combat operations. This was the most of any marine battalion in the conflict. Third battalion lost 653 marines during the Vietnam war and sustained over 2,800 wounded.

De-Vietnamization

We had been told that in order to qualify for the pullout, you had to have less than six months of duty left on your twelve-month tour, but that was not the way it worked out. Things seldom go as smooth as they're supposed to, and this was no exception. Once we settled in at Quang Tri, we were ordered to get our gear cleaned up because we would be pulling out and leaving for the States soon. Weapons had to be cleaned, inspected, and put away for the trip home. It was an environment of excitement as everyone started writing their families and telling them we were leaving Vietnam a little sooner than we expected. We would be home in a few weeks, and we were excited about getting out of this country alive.

Too Good to Be True

In September 25, we were called out into a formation to have a memorial service for those who had died on Operation Idaho Canyon. It seemed to be a lot of rifles with helmets on top of them, symbolizing the death of our friends. We were still reeling from the trauma of the operation, and the ceremony, though necessary for closure, was really depressing.

As the service ended, our sergeant major jumped up on a platform and started telling us about the pullout and how it was going to go down. About a dozen names were called out and told they would be boarding a ship in the next couple of days to formally escort our battalion flags back to the States. A few more details were given, and then to our surprise, we were dismissed. We looked at each other and thought, *Hey, what about us?* No one else had been included in any of the details of the pullout.

The Details

After waiting around for a few minutes and finding the sergeant major alone, I asked him about the rest of us. When do we leave? His answer stunned me. He told me that President Richard Nixon had called 3/3/3 back home, but now we were part of the First Marine Division. The First Marines in the south had recently taken a lot of casualties, and they needed experienced marines to help refill their ranks. Rather than using fresh, untested troops from the States, we would be reassigned to them. We felt like we had been snookered all along. We hadn't been cleaning our gear to go home. We were getting ready to go back into combat.

I went back to our squad tent and dropped the news on them. When they heard the update, they hit the ceiling. They were cursing, kicking, and throwing everything in the tent. We agreed we didn't know why it had hit us so hard. We shouldn't have been so surprised at the final outcome. We'd all felt like something would happen at the last minute to prevent us from leaving, and it had. It had been too good to be true. Renfro said they weren't going to let any of us go home until we were all dead. We laughed at his comment and agreed that he was probably right.

We started writing our families at once to cancel any plans for a home coming celebration. My dad told me later that he'd written the local newspaper in New Bern, telling them the troop pullout was a scam. His son had been with 3/3/3 for eight months, but recently, he'd been reassigned to the First Marine Division. Although the Third Marine Division was leaving Vietnam, we were still there. President Nixon may not have even known about the redeployment of units like 3/3, but he was the one bragging about us returning home on his watch.

Vanishing in Plain Sight

Within days, we were split up and redeployed into other units throughout the country, simply disappearing into oblivion. According to the media back in the States, there was going to be a big parade at Camp Pendleton, California, in the next couple of weeks for the media to see all the marines marching behind our flags appearing to be us, returning from Vietnam. The only problem was, the numbers of US personnel in Vietnam should have dropped dramatically but didn't. Most of us were still there, and President Nixon would get credit for bringing 3/3/3 back home The only things coming home was mostly our flags and the nongrunts it took to move our gear back to the States. After what we had just come through, it made me feel sick to think about the real possibilities of our going back into combat again, but that's where we'd be heading.

Bronze Star

As we were sitting around in our squad tent on the following day, an office POG came walking in with a clipboard in hand and called out my name. Raising my hand, he came over to me and sat down on the cot next to mine. "Clark, you've been awarded the Bronze Star for what you did up on the ridge." I was shocked. He then told me he needed to know exactly what had happened so he could write up the commendation for the award. I hadn't given it any thought as to any one particular thing I'd done in the firefight. It had been like trying to beat out a forest fire with a shovel, doing whatever we had to do to get it out. He questioned me again, "Can't you remember anything? You must have done something, or they wouldn't have put you in for this medal." As I tried to think of something to tell him, I asked if Bob DeRusso had received a medal for his actions up on the ridge. He looked for his name on the sheets of papers on his clipboard and said no, he didn't know anything about DeRusso. I told him that Bob had done one of the bravest things I had ever seen anyone do.

He single-handedly crawled through an enemy ambush to find a wounded marine and dragged him back to safety. I added that he should get at least a Silver Star for his bravery. The POG then told me that I was the last one to get a medal, and there were no more. My heart sank, realizing what had to be done. Bob had shown more courage than anyone else, and he deserved the recognition.

I asked the POG to go back to the command post (CP) and explain the situation, asking them to give the Bronze Star to DeRusso instead of me. He said, "Okay, if that's what you want." With that said, he walked out. Knowing that my chance for promotion to corporal, for the second time, had just gone out the window, I wanted to kick myself. My dilemma was simply knowing that if I made the wrong decision, I'd always regret accepting the award and not rightly giving it to DeRusse. I decided that if the CP refused to change the recommendation they had initially made, I'd be more than happy to accept it. I found out a little while later they did award Bob DeRusso the Bronze Star, and he was promoted to lance corporal. Being glad for him to get the medal he deserved, I hated that my dad would never know about the two Bronze Stars I'd been awarded in combat along with the two meritorious promotions I never received. It was merely a case of seeing where others had done greater things than I had, and it was hard to let them go unrewarded. I'm sure my dad was proud of me anyway.

Individual Redeployment Comes

The next afternoon, we were told to line up in front of our tents with all our gear. Our names were called, and we were separated into small groups. We were then told to move over to a corrugated airfield where we would board helicopters taking us to our new home down south. Several of our squad members went over to one area and sat down. We were in a daze as we watched the choppers loading up and taking off, knowing our turn was coming. I felt totally beat up. It was starting to get dark when a helicopter landed near us, and DeRusso and I were told to get onboard. We told Renfro and Taylor to take care as we walked off, not knowing if we'd ever see them again. We boarded the CH46 helicopter and took off, leaving Kilo Company and our friends we'd suffered and bled with behind.

During the noisy, dimly lighted helicopter flight, I leaned back against the bulkhead and closed my eyes as I began to think back... Everything had ended so quickly. The platoon of marines who had become a family had seemingly vanished in the past week and a half. Where was everyone? How many had died? Where were the seriously wounded taken? How many of us were left? There were so many questions and so few answers.

My brain began shutting down as I began to feel like a child again whose family had been torn apart and in my case for the second time. With my eyes closed, my mind began to recall memories of another time.

My mother had died from breast cancer in 1960 at forty-two years of age. She and Dad had been busy raising seven children with me being number 6 at eleven years old. Paul, number 7, was five years younger than me, and everyone else being at least five years older than me. Within six months of my mom's death, all my older siblings had left home to start their own lives. Dad was forty-seven years old and left alone to finish raising Paul and me. After everyone had left, the three of us moved from New Bern, North Carolina to St. Petersburg, Florida, to start life anew. Dad tried his best to help us in every way, but it was hard to adjust to our new life without the other six. In such a short time, everything in our lives had abruptly changed. The pangs of abandonment that tormented me in those days had returned, and now the knife inside of me just twisted again.

My New Home

The marines that I'd been with for over eight months were being split up and leaving all their experience of fighting the NVA in the mountains and jungles of Leatherneck Square. They were now going down to the First Marine Division in the south where the enemy looked and fought differently from their NVA counterparts. The terrain was basically a huge expanse of working rice paddies, which was also different from what we were used to. We were essentially having to start over with people we didn't know anything about, and in combat, that's never a good thing.

Shutting Down

My memory of being with the First Marines Division is very limited. I have no memory of the unit I was assigned to nor of the men I served with down south. My mind shut it all out as it seemed to have closed down on personal issues such as names and faces. Only a few firefights are in my memory, but that's about it. Isolating myself from making friends became part of my self-defense mechanism, protecting me from losing more friends. I do remember that in the first week of December, we came out of the bush for three days of rest and relaxation at China Beach. We arrived at a compound near the ocean and were taken into a fenced in area where we would spend the next three days of eating and drinking ourselves into oblivion. The first thing they did was take away our weapons, ammo, grenades, and anything else that went *boom!* They then read off to us all the rules they strictly enforced for the beach area.

1. No officer could come within ten feet of an enlisted man for the full three days and nights.

2. 2. We couldn't be seen at any time, day or night, without a free beer in each hand.

3. 3. There would be food provided twenty-four hours a day and movies each night until 02:00 hours.

You could ask for a cold beer, and they would give you a case. It was just what I needed to help kill myself!

One of the guys in my squad, who I'll call James, had gotten hold of some pot, and with all the free beer we had available to us, we commenced getting blown away. Soon, I became totally wasted and crawled off to myself to continue the destructive behavior throughout the night. At one point in my binge, all the anguish and grief inside me started to come out as the tears started to flow. Some thought it was the beer and dope causing me to act like this, but it was the pent-up emotions that had been boiling up inside me for months. It was sometime in early morning when I came to myself and stumbled back into our tent to start all over again. The food they were giving out never interested me as I don't remember eating at all. The weed and beer kept me crawling everywhere I went for the entire three days. There didn't seem to be any help for what was wrong with me because this thing wasn't fixable.

In my drunken state, I thought it would have been easier if I had died with them up on the ridge rather than living with the guilt of surviving without the others. I wanted to be with them in death rather than being with these guys in life. It was like dying a slow death on the inside and not being able to get any relief from it. The dope and alcohol was just making it worse. I must have been having a good time because before I knew it, we were on our last day at the beach, and my last night for getting blown away. We would soon be leaving for an obscure piece of real estate called Mortar Valley. Even the name of that place didn't sound friendly, but at least, we would get a chance to shoot at somebody.

About midmorning, the thought occurred to me, "Why waste a good day of drinking?" After finding my one friend, James, with the pot, we started getting drunk on our government-funded party and continued until late that night. The outdoor movie would soon be ending, and my buddy was helping me finish up the bag of weed. It was our last party before moving out in the morning, and we were making the best of it.

At 02:00, the movie ended, and everyone started back to their tents. It was really dark between the theater and the tent area, and as we were walking, talking, laughing, and holding each other up, we came up on a hole that someone had dug as a fighting hole or something. It had trash, pipes, and wood slats in the bottom of the pit, and stumbling through the darkness, I took a fall. As my right arm connected with a pipe, I felt it snap. James helped me up, and we looked at my arm in the light. It was broken at least in three places, and I was sobering up quickly. I looked deformed as my forearm had a huge U shape in the middle of it. I was in a daze, but then, it started throbbing like crazy. We stumbled over to the officer's tent and hollered for help. They all poured outside to see what was going on, and when they saw me, a corpsman was summoned. He checked out my arm as he called for a vehicle to take me to the hospital. The company gunny thought I might have broken my arm on purpose until I told him to go and check the hole for himself. He sent someone over, and they came back and reported that there was a hole with pipes in the bottom of it. The gunny got hot at whomever had left the hole like that and said he would take care of the marine that was responsible. He apologized for the self- inflicted comment he had made.

My platoon commander came out of the officers quarters and told me to "take care, Clark, and I'll see you later." He told the others to back off because I was a good marine who would never intentionally hurt myself. He and I had become somewhat friends during my short stay as he found out about my prior experience in the DMZ. I tried to help him in the bush because some of the peons in the platoon were taking advantage of him because of his inexperience. They were trying to get over on him by taking the easy way of patrolling instead of the safe way. If a certain way wasn't convenient, they would take the path of least resistance even though it might walk them into a possible enemy ambush site. That scared me because I'd been caught in too many ambushes already, and I didn't want to get caught in any more. He acted like he appreciated my help and moved me into his CP where I didn't have to go out on ambushes and patrols anymore. Unknown to me at the time, I'd never see anyone in the platoon again. If I'd known that earlier, my bullet-riddled helmet would have come with me. I had left it on my cot, and probably someone else took it home and showed everyone how they narrowly escaped death. A short time later, a truck came and took me to a real hospital with nurses and everything. I hadn't been near a real bed with sheets since my bout with malaria. The corpsman wheeled me off to x-ray where they informed me that my arm was broken in three places. They tried to set it but were unable to align all three breaks. They put a cast on it and then took me to a soft, clean bed with a pillow. Even though all the effects of the beer had worn off, no pain medicine was given to me because of all the alcohol I'd consumed throughout the day.

I was in full hangover mode and a little down on myself for having this happen to me until a corpsman told me I'd soon be leaving for Japan. Instant relief! It was over, and I had lived through it.

Before leaving country, I ran into Larry Renfro. He was at the hospital for trench foot he'd picked up in the rice paddies. He hadn't seen anyone from Kilo Company either and just wanted to get back home. He was still suffering trauma from the ambush as bad as I was, and his never-ending war would be just as severe. After that meeting, it would be almost another twenty years before I would see Larry again.

The following day, a group of us were flown from Da Nang to Japan on a C130 transport plane. Looking out the back of the aircraft, we could see Vietnam disappearing behind us. I could hardly believe it was over. The nightmare I'd been living through had ended, and I was going back to civilization again where everything would be good, or so I thought. Most of my problems seemed to be depression that started right after the ambush on September 15, 1969. It was the way everything with Kilo Company had ended so abruptly. All my friends were gone in one day, and I had no clue as to where they were or the condition they were in. There were no answers to my many questions. As time went on, the anxiety and depression I was experiencing continued on and never really subsided. It seemed the only solution to my dilemma was to move on and forget it had ever happened. How? I could never forget my friends, and soon, it dawned on me that I'd never be able to escape my own never-ending war. I would be forced to try and live two lives. One would try to act as normal as possible on the outside while the other would be slowly dying of anguish and grief on the inside. Only God could help me now, and I was too embarrassed to go to him.

Life after Vietnam

After returning to the States and being honorably discharged from the Marine Corps in February of 1970, I settled in New Bern, North Carolina, to work with my dad until his sudden death in November of the same year. With his God-given task completed of praying me through my days of close calls and near misses in Vietnam, the Lord took him to his heavenly reward. He and Mom were finally and forever back together again. My dad was my closest friend and confidant, and he will always be missed. Losing him so early in my recovery stages from Vietnam seemed to compound the grief and agony I was having to deal with on a daily basis. After returning home, I was consumed with my experience in the bush of Vietnam as I tried to self-medicate with drugs and alcohol which only worsened matters.

Without realizing it, I found myself falling into the same type of trap my father had been ensnared in many years before.

About My Father, Ronald E. Clark

He had spent his early years suffering from the hands of a strict Bible-based disciplinarian father who beat and punished him for every sin and rule he broke. The harsh treatment during his young life had driven him away from Christianity and into a life of alcoholism. It had started out as teen social drinking and ended up in full-blown alcohol addiction that ruled his life. His child abuse would be passed on to his own children in the years to come.

It was 1939. He and my mom had met and married before they were twenty years old, and during the course of fourteen years, they had given birth to seven children. The children were mostly the product of a solitary life of poverty and drunken parties brought on by the constant drinking binges. My dad was not only a drunkard, but he was also mean to everyone around him. He seemed to enjoy arguing and fighting as he would force my mom to drink with him when there was no one else around to get drunk with. As strange as it was, the only things my dad picked up in his youth was a mean streak and his love for gospel music. He loved the old-time hymns.

Intervention Comes

When our family moved to New Bern, North Carolina, in 1954, my parents were compelled to rent, at least temporarily, a two-story house across the street from the Salvation Army Church on Queen Street. Even though they were not happy about it, our house had a front-row seat into their services of loud music being played at least three times every week. My dad would get drunk and sit on our front porch as he listened to a song like "Amazing Grace, how sweet the sound, that saved a wretch like me" and others like "Just as I Am" being played and sung to the top of the parishioners lungs.

In 1955, on a sunny Sunday afternoon in July, my parents had spent the day sitting on the front porch, drinking. They had consumed the most part of a fifth and two pints of alcohol during the day as it would be his last binge before going to work on Monday. Dad worked as a painter and handyman for Maola Milk Company, and through that, he would bring home a sundry of milk products for our family. The ice cream treats also helped keep us occupied while they got drunk. On this occasion, he had brought home some strawberry ice cream for us kids. We had asked him for some, and as he was sitting on the front porch, scooping the ice cream into cones, the pastor, Captain Kenalogg, came out of the church and unlocked the front doors for the evening service. My dad spotted him and hurriedly made an ice cream cone for him. Dad stumbled out into the street and called for the pastor to meet him and take the ice cream treat he'd made. Captain Kenalogg graciously thanked my dad but said he couldn't stop because he had to start the church service in just a few minutes. Dad threw the ice cream cone into the street and cursed the pastor. He waddled back over to our house and announced to us that we were to "never go back across that street, ever again!" If we did, we would pay a heavy price for disobeying him.

As he sat on the porch simmering, we heard the music start playing for the evening service. My mom came out of our house, carrying my one-year-old brother, Paul. Dad told her to get us all ready because we were going to church. Everyone knew he was mad, and the only reason he wanted to go to church was to start trouble. He was probably going to end up in jail before the night was over, and Mom knew we didn't have any money to get him out on bond. He might even lose his job if he got locked up again. Dad promised he would behave himself as Mom got all of us washed up and dressed. Pretty soon, we formed up on the front porch and headed across the street to church for the first time. As we entered the sanctuary, there were two men standing just inside the front doors guarding the service from those who would disrupt things. Upon seeing our whole family, along with our drunken parents, they seated us toward the back of the church where they could keep an eye on us. I'd never been in church before, and the sanctuary seemed huge to me. Everyone was singing, clapping their hands, and worshiping God. It was different, but it felt good to a six-year-old. My parents acted like they didn't know exactly what to do as they just hung their heads and remained quiet throughout the robust worship service.

Then It Happened

Sometime during the service, while the music was still playing, the pastor came back to where we were sitting and began greeting and hugging on our family. Several others joined him as they began loving all over us. I looked down the aisle we were sitting and saw my parents crying for the first time in my life. My dad was really weeping as all the bitterness, anguish, hurt, and sin began rolling off of him. He and my mom stood up and started down to the front of the church were the altar was. A crowd of people gathered around them as they turned their lives over to God through Christ Jesus. They asked God for his forgiveness and to come into their lives and make them whole, and he did. From that night on, neither my mom nor dad ever drank another drop of alcohol again.

Our family was forever changed as we began a new chapter in our lives as my parents began following Christ through the ups and downs of life.

We began going to church at least three times each week along with other related activities. We went from a destitute, alcohol-controlled family to one that seemed to be living the American Dream in just a matter of months.

Six months after their conversion, they purchased their first home. Dad got his driver's license back and bought a car to carry us back and forth to church. All our friends were Christians who would have a get-together after Sunday night services where we ate, talked, and laughed. It was great.

My dad started his own painting business, and there was plenty of money to take care of our family needs as God was blessing us for our parents' dedication to him. Dad was a perfectionist at his job, and pretty soon, there was no shortage of work for him. At times, the work would be dangerous when climbing on ladders or scaffolding. If any of us boys would be scared and hesitate going up the ladder, Dad would always tell us, "Don't ever ask a man to do what you are too scared to do yourself." Then leading us by example, he would begin to go up the ladder. By the time his foot had stepped on the second rung of the ladder, we would push him out of the way and begin the ascent ourselves. He would smile as

★★★

he carefully watched us climb the ladder. That little saying of his caused me a lot of problems throughout my life.

Tragedy Strikes

In 1959, Mom was diagnosed with breast cancer, but our family's faith in God remained strong. She battled the cancer for over a year, but on December 28, 1960, she succumbed to the disease, and at forty-two years of age, she went to be with Jesus. Her death shook our family. We kind of circled the wagons around Dad and hung on to each other until we could adjust to life without her being with us. It was really hard to get used to. She had been a type of lynch pin that held our family together. We didn't realize how much she did for us until she was gone.

Six months after her death, Nellie, Virginia, Ronnie, Bob, and Jim left home to start their own lives. The only ones at home now were Dad, Paul and I. We had a large house with a huge dining room table that was able to accommodate twelve people, and now there was only the three of us at home. The house was too big to keep clean, and there was no reason to stay there any longer. A short time later, Dad decided to sell it and move. Through the encouragement of my sister Nellie who was living in Tampa, Florida, we not only moved from our big house, but we moved to St. Petersburg, Florida. The three of us would start our new life as a three-man family in a two-bedroom house.

Our New Home

Dad found a church nearby for us to attend and helped us get settled in at school. It amazed me as to how he made so many things fall into place with what we needed. It was like he was really smart and knew what we needed. He did the best he could, filling in for Mom in her absence. Even though he had plenty of temptations and excuses to go back, he never touched any alcohol again. He was finished with that lifestyle, and we were glad. We had enough problems without that one.

On one occasion, I saw Paul lying on his bed and quietly crying. I went over and sat down beside him. We hugged and comforted each other for a few minutes as we got out a little of our grief. He asked me, "Ray, why does it have to be like this?" My great words of wisdom back to him were, "I don't know. We just have to push on and help Dad out as much as we can. He doesn't need any extra trouble from us." That was the only time we ever really talked about our new lifestyle. I later bought him an acoustic guitar for his birthday. He learned to play and developed a love for music. Eventually, with better instruments, he became an accomplished musician that played the guitar, banjo, fiddle, piano, organ, and trumpet. He always credited me with getting him started in music, and in turn, he tried to get me interested in music too. I told him that playing a guitar had two requirements. One was talent and the other was desire. I lacked both, and it turned out that the only thing I could play on my own was a radio.

Many times I remember lying on my bed and thinking about my older siblings. Where did they all go? What happened to them? Were they okay? Did they ever think about us anymore? Would we ever see them again? There were no answers to my questions. Amazingly enough, these same type of questions would come to me again after the ambush of September 15, 1969. My marine family had been decimated, and again, I was left alone. When my dad died in 1970, it seemed to be the last straw. Disconnecting with people seemed to be the safest way to go. If you don't get too close to anyone, it doesn't hurt so badly when they leave. And they will leave.

My dad was a quiet Christian who read his Bible and prayed every morning before work and at night before he went to bed. He was resolute in his love, devotion, and worship for the God who had saved him and changed his life in such a positive way.

Because of my dad's love and faithfulness to him, the Lord was faithful to my dad. He heard his prayers in my behalf and delivered me even though my dad didn't have a clue as to when or what was taking place in my life. I'm a testament to the power of my dad's prayers to a loving God who hears and answers in behalf of his children. Thanks be unto God! Amen.

In May of 1970, I married a girl, Lynda, that I'd only known for a couple of months and tried to start a normal life like everyone else. The problem seemed to be that I was no longer normal. Throughout the year of 1969, I was being hunted by armed men that wanted nothing less than to kill me; and through that concept alone, it had somehow changed me emotionally. I stayed keyed up and hypervigilant all the time, never knowing when the enemy would show up again.

I had reentered society a different person and was now forced to pretend it had never really happened. The fact was that in the quiet of night my thoughts and dreams continued keeping me connected to my past as it seemed like the only life I really belonged to. I couldn't get away from Vietnam. I had no control over my dreams, and they were a constant reminder of how I'd participated in the killing of many men in various ways. Moving on in life seemed to be a little harder than what we'd anticipated it would be. It was harder than it was supposed to be... Vietnam was over, and I was home. All the hard stuff was behind me now, and the rest of life would be gravy.

But was it? The truth was that I would no longer have the luxury of being able to kill my enemy and get rid of him. It turned out to be the worst villain for me to fight was the enemy within. PTSD seemed to be stronger than me, and I didn't know how to fight it. When I'd start thinking about one of the firefights we were involved in, it would be like watching a video. Once it started playing, I couldn't cut it off because I wanted to watch it all the way through. I was proud of the accomplishments Kilo Company had made in 1969, and I was proud to be a part of them. I belonged to those men to which I had such a great bond. We were forged together by deadly combat.

It was frustrating to me that no one had ever heard about the heroes I'd known in battle and didn't act like they were too enthused about learning about them. It was a total disconnect between the two worlds of war and a wimpy society I was now living in.

During hunting season in North Carolina, I would hunt deer and bear as a way to reconnect with my memories of the outdoors in Vietnam. I wanted to somehow continue being part of that world, but my combat experiences came back to haunt me in a negative way. After several years of struggling with the constant fear of being ambushed, I had to give it up. The shadows and noises of the woods caused me to think the enemy was hiding behind trees as I would become paranoid and jumpy just before going home to my unsuspecting wife and children. I'd already be keyed up when I got there. Lynda and I stayed together for ten years, and during that time, we had two sons, Mike and Eric. Throughout that time, I was silently suffering and dying on the inside while building walls up around me on the outside. Although I wanted to be a good father and husband, my drinking and emotional turmoil could not be hidden from my family any more than me trying to hide an elephant in an open field. Vietnam had changed me in a negative way and all who got close to me would suffer from my learned personality traits of temper, impatience, and strict discipline. All those things were necessary in combat to keep men alive, but in peaceful family situations, they would ultimately end up destroying relationships. No one was able to measure up to the standard I demanded of them.

A Life-Changing Event

In November of 1980, I attended a revival service at my brother Bob's church because I needed help, and there seemed to be nowhere else to find it. I went there, knowing it was going against everything I'd been doing throughout the past ten years, but it was time for a change. In that service, I ended up asking God to forgive me of everything I'd ever done. He did and I was spiritually born again. It was like someone had turned a light on in my heart and mind and a ton of weight was lifted off of me in an instant of time. In Christ Jesus, I found an intimate friend who set me free from a heavy burden of guilt I'd been carrying around for a long time. He also promised to stay with me and never leave me alone again. He has kept his word and been faithful in supplying my every need throughout the past thirty one years, and I believe my eventual treatment with the VA was part of his plan for me to receive added emotional help and healing. Jesus has been a true friend who has given me peace and joy in every situation, and all I had to do was trust and obey him even through the difficult times. He didn't promise me the road would always be smooth, and it hasn't. He just seemed to put shocks on my wagon to absorb the bumps along the way.

Collateral Damage

Even in the light of my conversion, the problems of my past had produced permanent damage to my marriage, and it seemed to be irreparable. Although I was changing for the good and promised to do better, Lynda didn't want to continue with me any longer. She gave up trying and left me in 1981, taking with her our two boys. I would begin living by myself again, and it would be the third time for me losing my family. This time it was my fault.

In 1982, Lynda's divorce became final; it was hard not having my sons around and my untreated post-traumatic stress disorder was becoming a constant battle. Although I'd become a Christian, I tried to hide my emotional problems brought on by deadly combat in the meat grinder, and my memories were becoming harder to live with. God had forgiven me, but he didn't take away my memory. I tried to not think about combat or my lost friends, but little triggers would constantly cause me to think back to some ambush or battlefield I had been involved in. A sporadic attack of anxiousness or depression would suddenly come upon me, and I would have to isolate myself until they passed. Life alone was almost unbearable at times. On the outside, I was living in denial about my mental problems, pretending nothing had ever happened and everything was all right. I thought that if I remained silent about my past, my Christian friends would never know what a cruel, merciless murderer I had been in Vietnam. I was sorry for what I'd done to so many people, and I didn't know how to fix it. On two occasions, I tried to take the easy way out, but was interrupted at the last minute. I missed my friends and wanted to be with them in life or death, and it didn't matter to me which way.

If it hadn't been for the stabilizing force of Jesus Christ in my life, I would have never made it through those days. Unknowing to most people around me, I would get upset for no reason and start to hyperventilate. Within a few hours, I would snap out of my depression and push on without anyone ever knowing about the struggle I was going through. Christians were not supposed to whine or complain, and I just kept my mouth shut so as not to look like a whiner. I didn't ask the Veterans Administration for help because I was never wounded physically, and it would have been hurtful for them to tell me I didn't deserve help. I just sucked it up and kept on moving while keeping it all bottled up inside me. One thing my struggles did do was help me to pray more. I heard one preacher say that he had never prayed for thirty minutes, but he'd never been thirty minutes without praying. I thought that was a good idea and tried to do the same thing myself. It's helped.

Conformation of God's Intervention

In 1982, while working with my brother Jim, he began talking about some of the days he had worked with our dad during the time I was in Vietnam twelve years earlier. Jim had to be at Dad's house every morning at 05:30 sharp to start work. He said that Dad had a routine of always doing the same thing at the beginning of every work day. As Jim walked into Dad's house, he would always find him eating breakfast, reading his Bible devotions, and praying. As Jim spoke, the time of 5:30 a.m. caused my mind to go back to my personal ambush on September12, 1969.

The ambush had occurred between 17:00 and 17:30 in Vietnam as we were stopping to make camp for the night. My helmet was shot off my head, and I had to play dead for about twenty minutes to keep from being shot again and possibly killed. Could it have not only been a miracle but an actual intervention from God through my Dad praying for me?

> If any man see his brother sin a sin which is not unto death, he shall ask, and He shall give him life for them that sin not unto death. 1 John 5:16

This verse speaks of God hearing his children's prayers and answering them as he extends life even to the unsaved—me. Upon getting home that afternoon, I could hardly wait to call the telephone information operator and ask them the time difference between North Carolina and Vietnam. It was astoundingly twelve hours difference. That meant at the same exact time I was being ambushed ten thousand miles from home, my dad was praying for me. Coincidence? I don't think so. I couldn't help but wonder how many other times my dad was praying when the Grim Reaper was sneaking up on me. We'll never know, but more than likely every time.

It also occurred to me that my dad and I never talked about my near-death experience on September 12, 1969. He never knew about the ambush I was involved in, and I didn't remember about his daily prayer time. The important thing was that God knew about both of us and what was taking place in our lives at the same time. Dad prayed, God heard, answered, and I came home. Amazing!

Life Changes Again

After living alone for four years, in 1985, Laura Hardison Manning and I were married. We had attended the same Church for years but had only known each other through church and related activities. She was married to a man named Sidney and had five daughters. I only knew her husband the last few months of his life. He was a new convert and eager to do as much as he could for Christ, trying to make up for wasted time. I remember him calling me to go on visitation with him. I got to see his tender compassion for the sick and the lost during our short friendship before him succumbing to cancer. It was almost eight months after Sidney's death that Laura and I just happened to be at a church function where we noticed each other for seemingly the first time. It was also during a difficult time of life for both of us. We were both alone, compatible, and needed company.

After that, everything just kind of fell into place. She had started a bakery business in her home, which eventually helped support their family after her first husband was diagnosed with lung cancer. After Sidney's untimely death, she continued her cake shop as a means of provision for her and the two younger daughters, Jill, fifteen, and Amber, seven, still living at home. Her three other daughters—Cathy, Teresa, and Cynthia—were grown, married, and out on their own. In late March of the next year, we started dating and eventually married in August 1985. A year later, her dream to open a full line bakery was realized. She opened her cake shop called Laura's Cakes, Candies, and Supplies with me joining her in the "art" department. I ended up closing my business and devoting my full time to helping make her business successful.

We continued working together for the next thirteen years until my PTSD finally brought my employability to a halt. Panic attacks were becoming a common occurrence on a daily basis. I would get upset and take off for two or three days without saying a word to anyone. I didn't know what to say because I didn't know what was making me want to isolate myself from everyone around me. My combat buddies were the only ones I wanted to be around, and I didn't know where any of my friends were. My resolve was to go out into the woods and pretend to hunt. Maybe that way it wouldn't look like I was losing my mind. Due to my ever-growing emotional problems of detaching myself from everything around me, we agreed that I should relinquish my co-ownership of our business and private matters. Everything we had in partnership was put solely into Laura's name. It was hard to let go of all I'd ever worked for, but I knew it was for the best to let it happen.

During the years of working together, we had created and developed another part of the business called Laura's Military Cake Toppers. It was an acrylic bridal couple, customized and hand painted with the groom's fully detailed, military dress uniform (lauras-cakes.com). We've now sold them in over forty countries.

Never Forgetting My Friends

With my problem of never completely getting over Vietnam or forgetting my friends, I began a quest in 1999 to locate some of the men from Kilo Company, First Platoon. I utilized the Internet, Marine Corps records, and other sources that were available to me. Since that time, I've been successful in finding twenty-two former marines and corpsmen with several being from my third squad. It was an impossible task to accomplish until the advent of the Internet, making a world's difference in locating someone. Since initially finding them, we've had a number of small reunions over the past eleven years and always look forward to having more in the future. We are an eternal band of brothers that still enjoy being together after all these years. In 2002, I finally went to the Veterans Administration, per advice of my buddies, for help with my PTSD. In 2004, they retired me for my stress-related "mental illness." Yes! Mental illness. That was a hard pill for me to swallow. God had forgiven and healed me of many things including my rashes from agent orange and the reoccurring dream of the ambush on September 15, 1969, but he didn't wipe away my keen remembrance of combat. He allowed me to keep that so maybe I can help others who have the same problem of PTSD for whatever reason.

I've been blessed with a good family: my wife, Laura, and her five daughters—Cathy, Teresa, Cynthia, Jill, and Amber—along with my two sons, Mike and Eric, from my first marriage. They, along with a loving God, will help me through the days of adrenaline rushes, flashbacks, and a world going crazy. With their help, I'll make it to the end where Corporal Bushey is still waiting for me at the top of the hill. He'll probably ask, "Hey, man, what took you so long to get here?" We'll laugh, saddle up, and move on together, finally ending and defeating our never-ending war.

Living with PTSD

George Santayana once said, "They who cannot remember the past are condemned to repeat it."

That being true, there is another line of thought that warns about those who dwell on their past will rob their own future. This is one of the many problems with post-traumatic stress disorder.

In late 2001, I had reached a low point in my life where I needed help with my ever-growing emotional battles. My younger brother, Paul, died suddenly in February of that year, and it devastated me. It was reminiscent of the loss I'd felt when one of my buddies had died in combat. The guilt was overwhelming as my thoughts were telling me that I should have been there for him but wasn't. He'd left without saying good-bye and that also made me mad.

Another problem I began experiencing was the result of locating about ten of our Kilo Company First Platoon members throughout the year of 1999. Our first Vietnam reunion was in June of 2000, and it was a great success, but the memories of my Vietnam experience were fresher than ever. With every former grunt I found, the old wounds that had been locked away for so long were being reopened by having to remember and relive the year of 1969 all over again. It was undoubtedly good being back together again, but there were consequences to our traveling back in time. The emotions I thought had subsided with time were actually lying dormant beneath my exterior facade and were waiting to erupt with a vengeance. I found myself being consumed with my memories as my nightmares were becoming more frequent and intensely violent. I'd wake up exhausted from fighting all night in my dreams. The high anxiety that accompanied the dreams would continue throughout the day, bringing on unwarranted fear and excitability to my tormented mind.

My panic attacks now seemed to be coming daily, and there was no relief in sight. I didn't know why these attacks were coming like they were, and the only explanation to my dilemma was I was losing my mind. I'd never felt so alone, but to keep from telling Laura and admitting that it was more than I could handle, I'd slip off to my workshop and sit alone in the darkness, hoping the panic feeling would ease away with time. I was dying and didn't care.

My marine buddies would call from time to time to say hello, and on one occasion, a machine gunner, Ronnie Thompson, called and insisted I get in touch with the Veterans Administration for help. I really didn't want to, but this seemed to be my only recourse, and I was at my wit's end. He told me there is nothing weak or shameful about asking for help when you need and deserve it. My greatest fear was that they wouldn't even talk to me, but going to them didn't seem to be an option any longer. I had to somehow find help for me right away.

After making a call and visiting my local VA representative, it was just a matter of waiting to hear from them. My first appointment was in July 2002 at the Durham VA Medical Center in Durham, North Carolina. That's when the ball finally started rolling in my favor. The first thing I did was to assure them there was nothing wrong with me. They assured me that I was in denial and needed to open up and let it all out. Being stunned at their invitation, I started talking about Vietnam, and pretty soon, my emotions began taking over about my anger, disappointments, and shame that had been buried for a long time. It all began to spill out of me, and it wasn't long before I broke down and started crying for the first time in a very long time, telling them how messed up I really was. They let me know they were there to listen and help me in any way they could. I could hardly believe the compassion these people were extending to me, and it reinforced the idea of my coming to the right place. I do believe that God was guiding me in the right direction.

In time, they explained to me that the sustained combat I was exposed to in Vietnam and the high stress level we lived in on a daily basis caused my adrenaline to pump at an unusually high rate. The excessive amount of adrenaline pumping had created a chemical imbalance that brought on a myriad of problems including panic attacks. It didn't matter how long it had been since the trauma. The chemical imbalance was not going away by itself, and it had to be treated as a brain injury or mental illness. I was not thrilled about having a mental illness, but it did explain a lot of things about me to my family.

I began finding out that it was not so much the memories of battle that was the source of my problems. It was the adrenaline disorder that was causing my emotions to run rampant with the same intensity or greater than they had once been in combat. It turned out to be a chemical problem in my brain that could be treated with the right dosage of pharmaceuticals. Great! Let's get started right away. In May of 2003, I was permitted to participate in a six-week program at a VA Hospital in Salisbury, North Carolina. During the six weeks of impatient care, a group of eighteen veterans were daily scrutinized and treated by doctors, psychiatrists, psychologists, and social workers. They used medications and group therapy in their clinical treatment to help with the emotional problems associated with the stress-related disorder. Everything provided by the VA Mental Health Professionals was intended to treat the emotional difficulties the veterans were constantly experiencing. The patients were encouraged to openly talk about their lives before, during, and after Vietnam. After the first few days of treatment, we began to calm down and open up to one another, allowing the healing process to begin working for each of us. I enjoyed the time spent at the hospital and learned many coping skills that I still use today. I recommend to any veteran suffering with PTSD to inquire about the program through their local VA representative. While there, my family was financially compensated by the VA, and the study worked greatly in confirming the validity of my PTSD symptoms. Within about six months, it led to my being granted a full and permanent disability status.

The VA's mental health doctors explained to me the many triggers that caused my adrenaline to rush uncontrollably. They included rain, thunder, loud noises, crowds of people, and even strong winds blowing, recreating the chaos of combat. When the adrenaline pumps for no apparent reason, the victim goes into a fight or flight mental state that is characterized by excitability, increased heart rate, irritability, and paranoia. The only natural course for the untreated victim to take is to isolate themselves until the attack passes. They are forced to live in a state of loneliness and depression, which can lead to suicide if untreated.

PTSD is not a new phenomenon. It's just an old disorder with a new name that's brought on by combat and other traumatic events. Those who fought in WWI, WWII, and Korea had the same symptoms, but their disorder was called by a different name. Shell shock, combat fatigue, and battle fatigue were some of the names that were used to describe their mental and emotional problems brought on by combat.

From my initial contact with the VA, they knew they were essentially working with a time bomb. PTSD had already been the possible cause for many thousands of veterans committing suicide, simply due to being untreated.

It was made clear to me in the beginning that there was no quick fix or silver bullet that would make the persistent symptoms disappear, but they could be managed if I would listen to what they said. The VA would teach me certain techniques that if followed, could help minimize my level of stress and tension. They furnished the tools to help in my recovery, but it was up to me to utilize them at home.

In Summation

I'm resolved to the fact that my never-ending war will never entirely go away, but I do believe forgiveness of our past can be accomplished through God's love and mercy if we will just ask him to. We in turn will have to ask for God's help in forgiving a lot of other people for their mistakes. The key to our success is forgiveness. It is said that the heaviest burden for a person to carry is unforgiveness. It will eat at us like a cancer if we allow it to go untreated. We've got to have peace for ourselves in spite of what others have done. Regardless of what has happened in our past, our future is spotless. God has given each of us the ability to pursue and enjoy the rest of our lives if we will just begin by reaching out to him first.

> This is called the Romans Road.

> For all have sinned and come short of the glory of God. (Romans 3:23, KJV)

> For the wages of sin is death; but the gift of God is eternal life through Jesus Christ our Lord. (Romans 6:23)

> Confess with thy mouth the Lord Jesus, that God [the Father] has raised Him from the dead, and thou shalt be saved. (Romans 10:9)

1. Admit you are a sinner in need of his salvation.

2. Believe that Jesus is Lord and Christ.

3. Confess your sinful state to him, and you shall be saved.

I have no doubt that God could have healed me completely from PTSD, but instead, he used my disability to allow others to enter into my life so we could end up helping each other. Quit worrying about what others will say about you and just do it.

Coping Skills

The art of survival in combat is to recognize your enemy and attack him at the right moment. My enemy has changed since Vietnam, but the battles of mental endurance continue to plague me on a daily basis. For this type of warfare, I've had to learn and develop coping strategies for defeating my new enemy called post-traumatic stress disorder. It is an unseen enemy that I have to fight vigorously in order to keep from succumbing to its deadly, suffocating tentacles of depression, self-destruction, and dysfunction. I survived Vietnam, and by God's help, I will survive the aftermath as well.

In this chapter, I've had to become vulnerable in taking a chance of looking like a wimp to many tough guys who think—like I once did—they are above seeking help. I may be a wimp, but I don't think so. First of all, I was once a tough guy who walked point in the meat grinder of Vietnam, and the tension of that experience itself helped cause a lot of my emotional problems. Some of the coping skills I suggest may not be manly enough for some, but they work for me, and I think it's worth the risk of me looking weak in order to help those who are suffering from PTSD. In order for me to do that, I've had to expose my hidden emotional life in a transparent way, graphically revealing my mental and physical problems and showing how I have gained relief from many of them. This is not something I would choose to do, but I've come to realize that there are many victims in the balance of life and death, and if they don't get help soon, they're going to die. I personally feel that if they will take heed to the information contained in this chapter, it can help save their life, marriage, and family from a life of turmoil.

An American Hero

One of my favorite American heroes has always been Audie Leon Murphy. He joined the army on his seventeenth birthday to fight the Germans in WWII and became the most decorated US veteran of the entire war. He received thirty-three combat awards and decorations including the Medal of Honor for conspicuous gallantry and intrepidity at the risk of his own life above and beyond the call of duty.

Unknown to many at the time, Audie suffered from what is now known as post-traumatic stress disorder and was plagued by insomnia, depression, and anxiety attacks stemming from his combat experiences. He fought going to sleep in order to avoid the nightmares of warfare where many of his friends had died in battle. There seemed to be little anyone could do for combat veterans like him, but he never gave up. He became an active advocate for the needs of veterans as he broke the taboo about discussing war-related mental health problems connected with PTSD. Audie Murphy spoke out candidly about his personal problems with PTSD also known as battle fatigue. He insisted the government give more study, assistance, and health care benefits to returning war veterans from Korea and Vietnam. He was a champion of warriors, and there will never be another Audie Murphy. We can all be glad he was on our side of the war. If an American hero like Audie Murphy can be humble enough to admit his being effected by PTSD, why shouldn't we follow his example?

As I began treatment at the VA for my disorder, I started learning about coping skills to use for my problem. It was surprising for me to find out that several things in the VA program were already in my daily schedule as I'm a survivalist in nature. The things that I was already involved in simply made me feel better

LM Clark

and were considered positive pass times. They were martial arts, motorcycling, easy listening/soft Christian music, and an active spiritual life. They helped reduce my aggression and tension throughout the day and gave me an outlet for my pent-up emotions that would have otherwise been simmering inside me. The VA not only recommended my continuing these activities, but their added suggestions enhanced the ones I'd already been doing on my own. Instead of surrendering to a life of panic attacks, I'd make myself get up and do something or go somewhere to keep me from just biding my time away, alone, and depressed.

A simple but immensely helpful trick in my arsenal of self-control methods is I made a two-by-three-inch brightly colored sign that simply says Light N Up. It sits on the dash of my car. If someone cuts me off in traffic or I get stressed out over some insignificant matter, the sign reminds me to get over it and move on. At the moment I want to rip someone's head off, I catch sight of the card and instantly calm down. It's amazing how much the sign helps to lighten up my day, and I don't have to go to jail for killing some idiot on a cell phone.

While writing my memoirs of Vietnam, I thought it would be remiss of me to tell of all the problems connected with life after combat without giving and expounding on some of my personal techniques that help me contend with PTSD from day-to-day. It is an ongoing disability that needs a daily dose of medication and self-maintenance, which enables me to overcome the depression and hypertension associated with the illness. Now that I know the problem and the cure, it is up to me to apply the right medicine in order to have a good and fulfilling life.

The list of tools that are in my arsenal are things that work for me. Some of my remedies are not for everyone because they are seen by many as different or dangerous such as riding a motorcycle. Most people either love or hate motorcycles. I just happen to be one that loves them. I feel comfortable riding my motorcycle in heavy traffic. It may be crazy, but I just sit back and watch the world go by. In such situations, my brain has a reason to produce adrenaline, which causes me to relax and enjoy the ride. Others may have lifestyle situations and disabilities that may limit them, and they cannot do the exact same things I do. They will have to come up with their own list of tools on a personal basis.

My personal coping skills are the following:

1. It's about staying busy. Whether I feel like it or not, I try to stay busy at home. That way my home stays in good condition and my wife stays happy. If I can't think of anything to do around the house, I'm sure she can.

    1a. I also have a hobby. I have found that through growing bonsai trees in my backyard, I gain personal enjoyment and satisfaction in creating a piece of miniature living art. It is a very quiet and creative pastime that brings a sense of peace and tranquility to me just as painting a picture would be to someone else. The difference is my art is alive and has to be fed, nurtured, and talked to just as you would a child. It depends on my daily attention to keep it healthy. You can find out more about growing your own bonsai on the Internet. It's a choice and for me, being inactive can lead to depression and a bad temperament. Some days, I'd rather stay in bed and be left alone, especially after a night of nightmares. I may sleep late just to put distance between my dreams and reality but force myself to get up and get moving. Some may not understand my problem and become critical, perceiving it to be lazy. Get up and get going is the best policy.

2. I have in the past and will always use the VA to help me. They are caring health care professionals that are there to help us. If someone applies and gets turned down, keep trying. Any help is better than no help at all, and our lives and future may depend on our persistence. We need to

give them a chance to help us because that's what they are there for. Everything there is to know about the cause, effects, and professional help provided for the veteran with PTSD and their family is located at www.ptsd.va.gov.

3. My attending church regularly is just part of my Christian experience. There is great peace and consolation in knowing that as long as I walk with God, I will never go lacking. I can always trust him for my family just like my dad trusted him for me. Being around other believers is also a great source of surrounding myself with good, positive people. God cares about what has happened to me in combat, and he wants me to not focus on what I was, but what I was meant to be. The people I hang around with have a great deal to do with my lifestyle and character. I need to choose my friends wisely because I will probably end up just like them.

I am now alcohol free. That was one of my major destructive lifestyle problems that almost destroyed me. While at a bar one night, before becoming a Christian, I made up my mind to quit consuming alcohol because I was tired of drinking away all my money, and I didn't even like the people I was partying with. Combat had seriously changed me from being like most carefree, tough-guy people. After that night, I never drank again. Since becoming a Christian, I enjoy being with people of like-minded faith who help me stay sober and out of trouble. I spend the extra money I save on things I enjoy doing rather than always having to buy my way out of trouble with the law.

4. I encouraged my wife, Laura, to get involved with my healing process. She is my best friend, and when I hurt, she hurts. She has been victimized by my problems, and she's been part of my healing. After living with me, she may also need treatment for PTSD as she too has

been affected by my symptoms. The VA has a program for spouses of PTSD patients so they can have a better understanding about the problem.

I've learned that a good marriage is not a 50/50 partnership. It has to be a 100/100 participation if it is to succeed and flourish. The divorce rate among Vietnam veterans is over ninety percent with many of them being married multiple times. With each divorce comes added pain and regrets to spouses and children, and I don't need any more regrets than necessary. That alone will help me have a happier and longer life. If Laura ever leaves me, I'm going with her.

5. Amazingly simple as it is, I carry a Vicks nasal inhaler with me as a quick fix for a sudden panic attack. If I'm in a department store and start feeling unnerved, I pull the inhaler out and give it a sniff. It helps clear my head and startle me out of my attack. The next thing I do is get away from the noise and cacaphony of the store until I feel calmed down again.

6. Rest is important.

    a. I requested that my primary VA doctor have me checked me for sleep apnea. Being deprived of much-needed sleep was causing me to stay exhausted all the time. It just added to the problems I was already experiencing. Being checked is only part of the process of feeling better and healthier.

    b. If you are taking sleep medication, make sure it is doctor prescribed, and avoid alcohol as it could become a deadly combination.

c. I avoid caffeine or anything else that stimulates my adrenaline system before going to bed. It is better for me to watch or read something good just before going to bed as it helps me to think good thoughts while waiting to fall asleep. Listening to relaxing music also allows me to take a trip without leaving the farm. I sit back and enjoy the ride.

d. I avoid late-night pain medications as it seems to hinder my sleep if I take it before bedtime.

e. Leave a night light on if it makes you feel better. The enemy is like a cock roach. They stay away when the lights are on.

f. A "furry" friend can be a good companion even if they can't take the place of a loving spouse. The positive side of them is they don't talk back. They are great alarm systems, and they give me something to take care of.

g. I also cut back on my portions of food and lost forty-five pounds in a year. For me, it came down to losing weight or giving up karate and taking up sumo wrestling. I couldn't imagine me pushing some fat guy around while wearing nothing but a pair of BVDs. I lost the weight.

7. I make myself take my medication, especially the one for anxiety, often referred to as my be-good pill. It helps calm me down so I will be nice to everyone around me. My family can't help what happened to me in Vietnam, and I shouldn't take it out on them just because they are the closest ones to me. My guilt complex causes me to mentally beat myself up at times. It is partly due to the

verbal beatings I inflicted on my children as they grew up. I loved them and did not mean to hurt them, but I did. Making the transition from squad leader in the meat grinder to father of two small boys was not written about in the Marine Corps Training Manual. I had a hard time adjusting to civilian life after leading marines in combat as I demanded perfection without question. My favorite saying in those days was, "Just do it!" Now I'm saying "Please forgive me."

8. In December 1990, I decided to start exercising to get back into shape. There was an opening in a karate school, and I joined the class. It was like killing two birds with one stone. I'd get into shape and learn how to defend myself at the same time. The instructor was a police officer, Ronnie Lovick, and he was teaching a hard style of martial arts called Okinawan Shorin-Ryu. It was a way of life to the Okinawan people who took it very seriously. I started right away and fell in love with it. The main philosophy of the art was to never give up. The Japanese armies of WWII studied this style, and it was one of the reasons the Japanese were so hard to fight as most of them refused to surrender. If you gave up, you were less than human and deserved to die. They also had no pity on prisoners of war that gave up. It has been something I've enjoyed learning throughout the years, and my present rank is fifth-degree black belt. I was also blessed to be inducted into the Eastern USA International Martial Arts Hall of Fame in 2008.

I've had the privilege of studying under great masters like tenth master Shimabukuro Eisu, ninth master Sam Pearson, eighth master Scott Warren, and seventh master Ronnie Lovick. We study and teach how to defend ourselves in every way of mind, body, and spirit. We encourage our students in character growth through reading the Christian Bible, such as the Book of Proverbs. One such verse tells us that

> "a soft answer turns away wrath, but grievous words stir up anger." (Pro.15:1, KJV)

We teach them to love and pursue peace but prepare for war. We also teach them from the masters. Master Shimabukuro tells us that with gaining ability, we must also have humility. He says,

> The stalk that bends the lowest has the most rice on it.

Because a person is humble, it does not mean they are weak. A little humility is far less painful than a lot of humiliation. By the way, Laura refuses to call me master even though I've achieved the rank status. That in itself is humbling. She tells me that she only has one master—Jesus—and I humbly agree. My students also give me a reason to stay active in teaching them the deep things of the art. I have learned much throughout the years about enduring from the art.

9. Motorcycles. Two things are necessary. They must be very loud, and they must be easily seen. I've added fog lights to my Harley Heritage Softail to give others better visibility of me. Pride is not the only reason you want to be seen by motorist. I've ridden for many years, and it has been a great source of pleasure and a way of getting away to blow off some steam. Riding in traffic at seventy miles per hour is relaxing to me as my adrenaline has a reason for pumping. If I'm having a bad day because of a nightmare and my adrenaline is pumping, I'll jump on my "hog" and take off for a couple of hours as my cares seem to melt away. The only way to stay safe while riding is to not let your mind wander off. Taking your thoughts off of the task at hand of staying upright is downright dangerous.

Riding provides a good time-out to settle my nerves. The wind is one of my triggers that possibly came from sitting out in the open during a typhoon in the monsoon season of Vietnam or not being able to detect the enemy in the jungle on a windy day. Oddly enough, the wind going past me while riding my motorcycle doesn't bother me at all. It actually helps to calm me down. It must be a control thing.

10. After being prompted by my VA therapist to do so, I wrote in detail about my worst experience in Vietnam. I wrote about the ambush on September 15, 1969, and thought I had done a great job in remembering it in such detail. To my surprise, instead of them being impressed with my accurate account, they told me to write it again with more detail. My reaction was "Do what?" Being shocked by their request, I questioned their motive of playing with my head. I couldn't help but wonder where this thing was going as they told me to just trust them. I reluctantly continued following their instructions. It almost became like a joke as they told me to write it again and again with more detail each time. I didn't like the idea of doing this assignment at first, but during the process, a strange thing started to happen. A lot of pent-up emotions I'd been secretly carrying around for a long time began pouring out. Bitterness, anger, remorse, regret, etc., came flooding out as I continued writing with more honesty each time. After a while, I noticed that the pain I'd been feeling for so long started to subside a little with each time I wrote about the ambush. Through the pain of writing and rewriting a battery of accounts, I was able to unload a lot of unwarranted guilt as I began to feel better for the first time in a long time.

11. Another helpful assignment was the VA therapist asked me about my feelings concerning the ambush on

September 15, 1969. Did I feel guilty or blame myself for what had taken place that day? Did I feel responsible in any way for so many of my friends being injured and killed? Why has the memory of Hill 410 caused me so much mental pain and anguish throughout the years? What degree of responsibility did I truly have over the events of that fateful day? In all honesty, I could answer all her questions except for the last one mainly because I had never really considered or thought about the responsibility part. When considering the facts, I was a squad leader and had very little to say about the operational decisions and objectives of the day. That was over and beyond my pay grade.

A Revelational Exercise

My therapist then asked me to draw a circle and take a slice out of it according to the amount of authority I carried that day. My sliver turned out to be little to none. Upon seeing how little influence I actually carried, most of the unwarranted guilt I'd borne for so long melted away, and I suddenly felt better about myself. I realized for the first time that I'd been a very small part of a much larger picture where my opinion mattered but little in the actions that took place that awful day. That simple exercise alone helped lift a heavy burden off of me. Everyone who went to Vietnam was wounded physically or emotionally and, for the most part, both. There have been times that I thought our friends who died there got the best deal as I slowly die from my war-related mental illness. As strange as it sounds and even though the NVA were our enemy, it seemed with everyone we ruthlessly killed, a little of us died with them. That kind of guilt only comes from being a young American that was raised to have morals and principals of decency and integrity. No country in this world is like America, and the young men and women we send to fight for freedom in a hostile world are the best we have. Killing our enemy was right, but the way we killed them was, at times, immoral. If we were fortunate enough to not get killed or severely wounded, we stayed long enough to get calloused. We hated the enemy and thought nothing of killing them in the harshest of ways.

We returned home and tried to become part of a society that had no clue as to what we had experienced in the war. We were not the same young men and women we had been before going to Vietnam. We came to belong to a unique band of brothers that stand alongside the greatest of American patriots that ever bled for and served our country. Personal sacrifice is what makes us different from the average American.

Those who fought in other wars had later returned home to a grateful nation and readjusted to civilian life again. We returned home to find that we had caused our country shame, and they weren't about to welcome us home. No parades, no job well done, no welcome home—nothing!

The generations of the 1960s and 1970s have finally faded away, and the following generations have replaced them. Today's school kids are appalled at the abuse and treatment we received, and they are embarrassed at what their parents did or did not do for the returning Vietnam veterans.

We have returned, somewhat readjusted, and settled in for the long haul. Today, America is proud of their fighting men and women in uniform and goes to great lengths to show their appreciation. We are now included in the long list of America's heroes, and it's good to be home.

In 2006, as Larry Renfro, Ronnie Thompson, and I were in Washington, DC, visiting one of the memorials. A lady and her young daughter approached us and asked for our autograph and thanked us for serving our country. We were surprised and humbled at their request. What an honor!

Our job now is to make sure everyone in the Armed Forces know that we appreciate them serving, and we are standing behind them in our thoughts and prayers until they have all come home. To everyone who has ever served our country in the Armed Forces, thank you. To those who supported our men and women in uniform throughout the years, thank you.

> John Milton said it best in his sonnet, "They also serve, who stand and wait."

Especially to the Vietnam veterans, thank you and welcome home!

A story to remember...

> An incident happened during a battle in the American Civil War where the Confederate forces were suffering heavy loses in a fight with the Union defenders. As the battle progressed, the Confederate general realized their dilemma and called on his bugler to sound retreat and pull his men back to avoid a massacre. He found his young bugler and commanded him to immediately sound retreat. To the general's surprise, the young man shouted back to him, "Sir, I can't do that."
>
> The stunned officer repeated his command with more fervor and desperation than before shouting that his men were being cut down like the grass. The young bugler only stood motionless as he seemingly didn't know what to do. The general then rode up to the boy and jumped off his horse. He grabbed hold of the terrified youngster and repeated his command of "Sound retreat. My men are dying out here."
>
> The bugler simply said, "Sir, I can't."
>
> The general hotly questioned, "Why not, boy? Why can't you sound retreat?" The young man replied, "Sir, you never taught me how." The shocked general shouted in desperation, "Do something, boy. Do something quickly!"

Being that the only song the young recruit had ever learned was "Charge," he began playing the battle cry as hard and loud as he could—over and over. Those on the front line fighting heard him and thought their reinforcements had arrived. They began fighting like wild men. The wounded that could still fight heard the bugle, and they too thought reinforcements had arrived. Standing up, they also rejoined the battle. The soldiers who had run from the fight because they were scared to die thought more friendly troops had arrived, so they ran back to rejoin the fight. The course of the battle turned that day and the Confederates won the victory because the youngster had not learned the song of retreat.

—Unknown author

We with PTSD are mentally wounded, bleeding, and beat-down. We feel like lying down and playing dead so everyone will leave us alone. We can't stop or give up because our enemy will have no mercy on us. We have to remember that there are many people fighting for us, and we can't let them fight alone. We have to get up and rejoin the fight. There is still some warrior spirit left in us, and we can't help ourselves or anyone else if we give up and retreat from the battle. Don't give up, retreat, pull back, let go, or run from the fight. PTSD is a battle we can win if we will face it head-on. Get the tools, the resources, and the will we need to beat it, and we can do this thing if we will push on.

Semper fidelis!

Where Did They Go?

In 1999, I began trying to locate the survivors of the September 15 ambush. With the help from the Internet and the Marine Corps Record Division, I was successful in locating twenty-two men from our first platoon. Along with that list came another forty marines from the rest of Kilo Company that our "Skipper" Captain Paul Goodwin had previously located. The VA was helpful but somewhat limited in finding many of these men because of the Privacy Act protection, and most have never sought assistance from the VA until recent years. It seems as if the grunts are the ones who suffer the most and are always the last to ask for help. The Marine Corps Records Division in Quantico, Virginia, supplied us with any two company rosters for any year we wanted. We chose September 1 and September 20 of 1969, so the names on the two lists could be compared. Everyone who had died on Operation Idaho Canyon was absent from the September 20 roster. We then could look on the Vietnam Memorial Wall website and find their name confirming their death.

The Rosters helped the VA to locate some marines through the names and service numbers posted on the list, providing they were already connected to the VA system. Medical records were obtained from many of the wounded on September 15, providing an exhausted list of casualties and extent of the injuries to all the wounded that day. We now knew that many of our friends we thought had died in that operation hadn't, and they could possibly be located with a little effort on our part.

All of the men I've located are fighters that have struggled with their injuries and memories of combat. It is amazing how they persisted on with life after the dramatic, life-altering experience of Vietnam had ended. After serving a year in a sustained combat zone, we lived through enough traumas to change our direction and future plans for the remainder of our lives. It would have been easy to give up years ago, but that's not who we are and what we did. The way these men have persevered in spite of their traumatic injury is a testament to their character and determination they learned in the jungles of Southeast Asia. Many of them were not even old enough to vote, but they defended the freedom of others at their own hurt.

It's been an honor and privilege to know such men as these, and as it was once spoken,

> Men are made from the neck up—not the neck down.

Your height or size does not matter when it comes time to go to war. These men heard the call and answered when it was not popular to do so, bringing pain and agonizing memories to themselves while standing in the gap for the next generation of freedom-loving Americans. They stand, philosophically, head and shoulder taller than most other men I've known in my lifetime. These men did not study the concepts of the philosophy of

> Greater love hath no man than this, that a man lay down his life for his friends. (John 15:13, KJV)

They lived it.

These are the men from first platoon that I've been able to contact:

- Larry Renfro settled in Lubbock, Texas, with his wife, Pearl. They had been married in Hawaii during his R&R stint. Larry was wounded two weeks after he returned to the company. He suffered with his facial wounds throughout the years but continued working until he retired, for the second time, in 2011. Larry had been successful in stuffing his memories of Vietnam away until

1990 when they returned with a vengeance. One evening at home, his memory suddenly recalled the sound of a helicopter passing overhead as he sat in his living room, watching television. The flashback caused him to suffer an unexpected traumatic breakdown. He suddenly realized for the first time in twenty years, it was not just a bad dream, but it had really happened. Larry was forced to begin treatment for severe PTSD that he continues today.

- Mike Mucyn married Pat in 1971 and had two daughters. He spent many years as an electrician with General Motors. He has constantly struggled with memories, emotions, and the physical wounds his received in the ambush on September 15, 1969. Mike worked two and three jobs at a time in order to squelch his mental pain he incurred in Vietnam. He sought help and was awarded one hundred percent disability from the VA in 2008. We met again for the first time in thirty-nine years at a 3/3 reunion in 2008. It was like we took up where we'd left off on that fateful September day. He is one of my closest friends. Mike told me he was in the hospital for a month, recovering from three bullet wounds he received on September 15. He was then released and reassigned to a new unit because 3/3 had pulled out of Vietnam. He went back into combat even though he did not have full use his right arm. He couldn't have thrown a grenade even if he had wanted to.

- Bob Snyder returned to Maryland and married Dee. They had two daughters. Bob had a hard time adjusting to life again as he went from one job to another. He never got over the pain, sadness, and anger he came to feel and experience in Vietnam. He tries to avoid talking about his tour of duty in Southeast Asia, if at all possible. He retired from driving a long distance truck in 2008 as his disability worsened. He continues to seek help from the VA for his emotional problems.

- Tom Rudisill went back to Michigan and started life again. He married but later divorced, as he had left Vietnam, but Vietnam hadn't left him. Tom was awarded the Silver and Bronze Star for gallantry but has had trouble in recent years getting help from the VA for his related PTSD. They insist he doesn't have a problem. He retired from driving a long-distance tractor trailer in 2010. Tom said that his greatest reward in life has been finding his buddies he served with and hearing them tell how much they appreciated his leadership in combat. He helped bring a lot of us back home.

- Dan Salles arrived back in California where he found America had changed during the year he was gone. Everything was distorted including the culture, music, and attitude toward the war. Dan had changed too. He was wounded three times and awarded the Silver Star, but no one cared. He quietly slipped back into society and tried to bury his memories and pain. Dan was married once and divorced. He had two children. He worked as a city building inspector and took early retirement from the city of Calabasas, California, in 2008. He is still in the process of seeking help from the VA.

- Ronnie Thompson located back in Delaware and married his wife, Micki. He worked as a steel fabricator until he had to retire due to his debilitating PTSD symptoms. He has continually struggled throughout the years with his nightmares and memories of combat. After many tries and attempts with the VA, he persisted and was awarded a full and permanent disability in 1990.

- Lt. Bill Haskell lives in Maryland with his wife, Charlee, and son, Zach. Bill was seriously injured in battle but has not allowed it to hinder him. He retired from his tax business in 2009 and annually competes in the grueling twenty-six-mile Marine Corps Marathon in Washington, DC. He has not only inspired me throughout the years, but he has also been a close friend. We ride our motorcycles every year in the Rolling Thunder Motorcycle Run on May 25. That is also the anniversary of his near-death experience on Mutter Ridge in 1969. Bill has always tried to help his marines whenever and however he can. He's still and will always be our lieutenant.

- B. J. Miller lives in Florida with his wife and has become a master jeweler over many years of working in the trade. He is currently connected with the VA for his wounds and PTSD he sustained in Vietnam. He is now retired.

- Bob DeRusse and Gary Kober attended our reunion in 1999 but have declined to participate in any others. The reunions bring up too much unwanted emotional pain for them. They will always be in our thoughts and prayers.

- Edward Cavazos lives in Texas with his wife, Lupe. They have two children. In 2011, Eddie is getting ready to retire from the aircraft industry where he has struggled but maintained his employment for forty years. He is now trying to seek help from the VA for his long-term mental health issues. He has been turned down four times for PTSD but still continues to seek assistance for his lingering problems associated with Vietnam.

- Doc Jerry Hrzic returned home to a quiet homecoming. He had multiple injuries from the battle at the riverbed in August of 1969. As he was being choppered out of the bush to the hospital, it was discovered that all the NVA weapons had plates on them telling they were donated by a well-known American university. Unknowing to Jerry, he ended up attending that same university in the early 1970s for a semester to study microbiology. He found out in 2008 that he'd been studying along side those who had supplied weapons to the enemy that had been trying to kill him. He was finally granted one hundred percent disability in 2009 for his physical and emotional injuries.

On August 11, 2010, Jerry called me and said, "Happy Anniversary!"

I questioned, "What Anniversary?"

Doc Said, "Forty years ago, you saved my life."

I laughed and replied, "Yeah, right."

My wife, Laura, was standing near me and had overheard me ask, "What anniversary?" She then went outside and sat down in a lounge chair on our back deck as if she was waiting for me. After finishing my conversation with Jerry, I went outside and joined her. She seemed a little aggravated as she asked me if Jerry had reminded me of my anniversary. I replied yes. She then asked me how he knew it was our anniversary.

I started sweating and said, "It was actually about our encounter forty years ago, but happy anniversary, honey!"

She looked at me suspiciously and said, "Tomorrow is our anniversary, but you need to call Jerry and thank him. You might have saved his life forty years ago, but today, he saved yours."

I promptly called and thanked Doc, telling him we were even. I'll probably never forget either anniversary again as long as Jerry is around. Thanks, Doc! He's still taking care of his marines. Jerry is also one of my closest friends.

- Doc Bill Rister was wounded twice. He resides in Louisiana with his wife, Sherri. They had three children. He's always worked in the medical field and will soon be retiring. Bill is haunted by the young men he watched die on the battlefield but is comforted by the many marines he helped keep alive. He's still seeking help with his ever-growing needs from PTSD. He and Doc Hrzic call their marines from time to time to see how we are doing. They will always be our docs.

- Eric Ritchey, James Grogan, and Edward Ham have all passed away in recent years before any contact was made.

- Lt. Eric Bowen lives in New York State and is married to his wife, Paula. He had two children from a previous marriage. Eric has spent the past forty years battling the eight wounds he received on September 15, 1969, along with the PTSD he incurred while leading marines in the meat grinder of Vietnam. He's had several operations on his legs as a result of the ambush. He continues to work even though his injuries cause him great discomfort. He will also forever be our Lt.

- Otis Taylor, who returned home to his mother and grandmother in Texas. He later married to Donna Jo and had two children. He stayed to himself and spent years going from job to job. He has been involved with the VA for forty years without receiving full benefits as of yet. He's still waiting.

- Wayne "Reb" Williamson lives in Mobile, Alabama, with his son, Hunter. He has suffered with his physical and emotional wounds for the past forty years. He worked on an oil rig in the Gulf of Mexico and with the State of Alabama until his injuries forced him to retire early. He has since been awarded one hundred percent disability from the VA.

- Jesse Abarca lives in Utah. He's been married for forty years and has five children. He has worked for the Aerospace Industry and, in later years, has battled PTSD along with the injuries he sustained in Vietnam. He continues to seek assistance from the VA.

- Doc Richard Hall resides in the mountains of Pennsylvania and works as a mechanic in a chemical plant. He still has his daily medical record book he kept in Vietnam, sending many of us to the hospital for one reason or another. He also has the bad fortune of having a sharp memory of his days in the bush and the marines he served with so long ago. He's struggling with PTSD on a daily basis and is trying to get established with the VA for future assistance. He took many pictures in Vietnam and shared them with us. They will always be a treasured record of our days in the bush.

- Lt. Richmond O'Neill lives in Texas. He has three daughters and a son from previous marriages. He has worked in construction for many years before retiring in 2009. He suffers severe PTSD from the memories of his days leading marines in Kilo Company as third platoon commander and later company commander. Richmond has always been a leader and still helps his fellow veterans in the local VA in Victoria, Texas. He is a great friend and a great marine.

- Aldo Torboli lives a quiet life in West Virginia with his wife, Susan. He drives a Tractor Trailer for USPS and is still trying to get established with the VA.

- There are many other former Kilo Company Marines including Paul Goodwin and Ollie North to whom I am eternally indebted. They helped me tremendously throughout the years and especially recounting this narrative in a more accurate way. To the men of Kilo Company 3/3, thanks and semper fidelis! To those who work in the Veterans Administration, thank you for helping us. We appreciate it more than you will ever know.

Elements of Support

As a marine grunt who spent over nine months in one of the most contested areas of Vietnam called Leatherneck Square or better known as the meat grinder, I, along with most other grunts, can appreciate the all inclusive value of fire support. On any given day, you could suddenly find out that the three NVA soldiers you just ran into were part of a company- or battalion-sized unit moving through your area. *Bam!* You're suddenly in a fight for your life, and you're outnumbered ten to one. What do you do? Call in reinforcements, ASAP. That scenario was not unusual to the men who fought the NVA along the demilitarized zone of Vietnam. Every day was just a new day in our tour of duty, and we never knew what it might hold as we were always in hostile territory. The average grunt in the DMZ of South Vietnam could see some form of contact with the enemy approximately 275 days out of their 365 days tour of duty. Life was intense along the DMZ.

Through daily search-and-destroy missions and major operations conducted in the region, Kilo Company was involved in many battles with the NVA but never without some sort of fire support. Artillery bases, off-shore naval gunfire from Big Mo, and air support were always there in a short amount of time to help bail us out of a bad situation. They were there with us throughout the pitch-dark nights with illumination, thwarting any plans the enemy had of over running our position. If they attacked, we would at least have visibility to see their forces coming at us and be able to counter attack them with deadly accuracy, keeping our lines intact until the morning sun would come up. If our support elements had not been there to help us, we would have been as helpless as the French were in the years prior to US involvement in Southeast Asia.

When in the heat of battle, the fighter jets would attack the enemy and keep them at bay while our medevac choppers dropped down to our perimeter to pick up our dead and wounded. Thousands of marines, sailors, and soldiers were saved from a painful and sure death by the bravery of the crews of the CH46 (Phrogs) as they came in amidst a fire storm of incoming mortars, small arms fire, and anything else the enemy could throw at them to knock them out of the sky. Every once in a while, we'd catch a glimpse of the facial expressions on the pilots and crew members as they came swooping in. By the look on their faces, they didn't want to be there any more than we did, but they continued coming in anyway. We knew they were there for us, and we were glad they were. The medevac choppers could usually be at the nearest hospital within forty-five minutes from taking off from the battlefield. It is estimated that ninety-nine percent of those who were alive when they were medevaced out of the bush lived because of the quick response and outstanding medical care they were given. The number of dead would have been dramatically higher if the choppers hadn't been there for us. But they were.

Different Types of Support

1. The CH46 (Phrog) twin rotor transport helicopter was extensively used as the work horse for the Marine Corps in Vietnam. They provided all-weather, day or night, assault transport of combat troops, including medevac, supplies and equipment. Assault support is its primary function, and the movement of supplies and equipment is secondary. They were found to be indispensable and highly admired by the troops on the ground. Former CH46 chopper pilot, General Tom Braaten, told me about him being a first lieutenant in Vietnam 1969. On one occasion, after returning from a mission into the bush, his crewmen

counted eighty-seven bullet entry holes into their chopper. That was just an example of the guts and commitment shown by all those who brought those birds into hot LZs to drop supplies to the grunts. They weren't thrilled about having to do that kind of thing, but they did it anyway. The only thanks they got in those days was a simple wave off, but it was more than a gesture. It was a thank you from one marine in need to another as the choppers were bringing us relief.

2. The HueyCobra gunships were with us in most battles, and we were glad they were on our side of the war. They were awesome to watch as they swarmed around the NVA like a bunch of angry wasps while the CH46s were picking up our wounded. Everyone worked together as a team, and it turned out good for us on the ground. The HueyCobras were multirole attack aircraft that used air-to-surface missiles—7.62-mm. mini gun pods, 20-mm. and 30-mm. cannon armaments, and 40-mm. grenade launchers. Their main role for the marines was covering support for troops and CH46s.

3. AC130 and AC147 (Lockheed) were commonly known as Puff and Snoopy gunships. They were armed with three miniguns that fired three thousand armor-piercing rounds per minute per gun. They also fired cannons and howitzers. They gained their lethality through support of troops in contact. They would fly over combat zones, looking for enemy light structures, light-armored vehicles, or enemy troop movement. The gunships bailed us out many times when heavily outnumbered by battalions of NVA around the DMZ. Puff would rain down death from above in the darkness of night as they fired their miniguns in close support around our perimeter lines. We would light our C ration heat tablets in the bottom of our fighting holes

to help them know our exact location, hoping we'd not become collateral damage. Their deadly fire would break up the attacking hordes of NVA troops, thus saving the lives of many young marine grunts below, by fighter air-crafts (fixed wing). Within the opening minutes of a fire-fight, Captain Goodwin would have our forward air controller summoning air support with "troops in contact!" The fighter jets would soon show up to drop their napalm on the attacking NVA. With their arsenal of cannons, bombs, and napalm, the grunts would soon be on their way of getting control of the situation. Our fight was face-to-face with the enemy, but we could have never done it in such a short amount of time without our fixed wing.

4. The battle tanks that helped us out on two different occasions were amazingly fierce in battle. We also learned a valuable lesson from an NVA soldier at Mai Loc that jumping beneath a moving battle tank is never a good idea. He was instantly chewed up into a ball of flesh and spat out by the tank treads. It was a bad way to die. Thanks to tankers like Capt. Mike Wunsch who gave their lives while helping us to live will always be remembered as heroes to the grunts. Words cannot express our gratitude and appreciation for their sacrifice.

5. The B-52 Stratofortress heavy bombers, the Cessna 0-1 (bird dog) spotter planes, OV-10 Broncos, our support bases, air crews, hospital men and women, doctors, and everyone else who put their lives on the line for us, *thank you*! We're home now because you were there for us then. Semper fidelis!

In summary, it's hard to explain what it feels like being on a lonely ridgeline in the middle of nowhere with a battalion of five hundred enemy soldiers surrounding your company of 180 men.

They knew where we're camped, but we're not sure where they're at. We did know they would be probing our lines throughout the night, and all we could do was stay ready for their attack when it came. The sun is going down, and it's getting dark. We feel very small and alone as everyone's aware it's going to be a long night. With all that said, we also know that our elements of support were with us and were waiting for our call for help. They would be on the enemy like white on rice, and there's some consolation and solace in knowing that. We could have never done our job if they hadn't done theirs. They did their job well, and many of us got back home because of the unsung heroes that flew in to assist us in spite of overwhelming odds of them being shot down. There are no words to express our gratitude for their sacrifice in battle better than the words *semper fidelis,* always faithful.

If someone stays in the military for any length of time, they begin to feel and experience a bond that nothing else in civilian life can substitute, even law enforcement or firefighters. It is the element of close military family life—a world-wide community of like-minded people who willingly place their lives on hold in order to protect us at home. They are deployed throughout the world where they put their lives at risk every day to keep our country safe and free. Military families are connected by a common mind-set of values, exceptionalism, and purpose. They are truly America's best. If you can spell, thank a teacher. If you can speak in English, thank a veteran. From the men of Kilo Company 3/3/3, thank you and semper fidelis.

Epilogue

The Writer behind the Scenes

My name is Laura, and I am the one who has helped my husband write this story. It has been a challenge and an honor to be part of this project as I have been able to learn more about the men of Kilo Company up close and personal. I normally love to read nonfiction about someone or something that makes me laugh or cry as I delve into the plot of the story. This project was simply listening to Ray tell of the bravery and antics of his friends as we both laughed and, at times, cried together. It was heartwarming in places and heartbreaking in others. The thing that amazed me most was that it was real, authentic, and-mind boggling to say the least. It was hard to believe that my considerate and thoughtful husband had been a participant in deadly combat for a year of his life. It was a total contradiction to what he is today and what I've always known him to be. I was amazed as I sat and learned what fear is really like when men are hunting each other down with one goal in mind—kill the other before he kills you.

Although it's been forty-one years since Ray has returned from the war, his feelings, memories, and emotions are still sharp and sensitive as he takes the reader into the daily life of a grunt in the bush of a third-world country. He exposes the reader to a graphic type of war narrative that can only be produced by those who have lived through it. While living in my comfortable world, I couldn't have ever imagined the daily grind involved with trying to stay alive for a year in a deadly jungle filled with leeches, mosquitoes, lethal heat, and an elusive enemy that was constantly trying to kill you.

Through writing this story, I was affected in ways that helped me finally understand the emotional numbness and depression Ray and his buddies have been experiencing for years. I have also found that for one reason or another, most of them have never told their stories to their spouses or families. They unintentionally cheated us from knowing and appreciating the heroics they bravely went through in Vietnam. This book has helped open my eyes to a world beyond my comprehension as I realized what these men are and have been feeling all along.

Disconnected

Before the beginning of this project, my disconnect from Ray's PTSD problem caused him periods where he had to suffer alone simply because I didn't understand. I had no idea of the depth of the problem he was silently dealing with as he would slip away and isolate himself from everyone. I could not identify with his stress-related disorder. Throughout my life, I've been a positive type of person who always thought the glass was half full, rather than half empty. Even through my first husband's sickness with cancer and eventual death, I pushed on with raising my daughters and never let anything get me down. I couldn't understand anything becoming so intrusive or overwhelming that it would burden someone so much of the time. I just didn't know about PTSD. When Ray and I married in 1985, he kept quiet about his memory and dreams. He was visibly hypervigilant in crowds, and he couldn't tolerate simple everyday pressures. I would criticize him for his lack of patience, and he would then say, "You're right! I've got one nerve left, and you're standing on that one! Back off!"

It was like he had closed off part of his life like a room, and he wouldn't let anyone inside to see what was going on. He was struggling every day in his own world as he constantly suffered silently and alone.

It seemed as though he progressively got worse as the years went by, but something happened at the beginning of the Gulf War in 1990 that caused him to start going downhill quickly. His dreams and flashbacks began to come back with more frequency and clarity. He missed his friends more than ever and wanted to be with them even though his platoon had been wiped out in 1969 and he had no way of knowing if any of them were still alive. He felt *alone*, and I couldn't do anything to help him, so I just stood by and watched him deteriorate. Ray always eliminated himself from treatment by the government because he wasn't physically wounded in Vietnam. From that alone, we never considered asking the VA for help because he didn't think he deserved it. Big mistake! In 1999, Ray began searching for and finding his buddies through the Internet. He was able to locate about twenty of them throughout the next seven years. Since then, we've gone to several reunions, and it's been amazing to finally meet many of these heroes I'd only heard about. It was obvious to see Ray was struggling with his memories, and many of his buddies picked up on it right away. Through Ronnie Thompson, former machine gunner, Ray was persuaded to contact the VA for help. In 2002, he was diagnosed with severe PTSD. Eighteen months later, he was granted a full and permanent disability for his stress-related disorder, PTSD.

The Book Finally Comes

In 2010, Ray and I took our first cross-country trip in a car that took thirty-four days. We looked at the beautiful mountains and plains, but much of it reminded him of Vietnam. As we drove and talked, we decided to start writing his story in-depth and with as much detail as possible, partly as a tribute to the men of Kilo Company. We'd start at the beginning and see where and how it stops. As we talked and wrote, we decided the most befitting name for the book would be *The Never-Ending War* because sadly enough, it will probably never end. We figured that even though it was a tragic story, there had to be something good in it that would come forth through our effort. It turned out to be healing and forgiveness that they all needed to obtain in order to gain peace along with the reunions that brought them back together again. The language of combat in the book has been somewhat sanitized in order to make Ray's story more readable and beneficial for everyone. There are so many people in this world that have been forced to isolate from family and society through horrific, traumatic events causing them to silently suffer, and we didn't want any of them to be eliminated from reading this story. We felt strong, abrasive language or sexual content would be counterproductive in reading through the entire book. It would also be out of character for us as being a Christian family. We hope that the coping skills Ray has employed in his daily routine will benefit anyone who is suffering alone with PTSD.

It's been a great honor for me to meet these former marines and corpsmen after learning about the sacrifices they made for our country. I never knew their true account until Ray told me in specifics of what really happened so long ago. I was amazed. The cliché tough guy begins to take on a whole new meaning when you meet these marines of Kilo Company. The likes of these men stand a head and shoulder taller than most other men I've ever met as they lived through what others only dream of doing. They still stand together as a band of brothers that were fused together in deadly combat—only now they have all our families to stand with them as we thank them for their accomplishments. Their children have told us at reunions that they never knew about their fathers' heroics in battle until these old warriors got back together again. The closed-off room in their minds has been opened up, and we, their families, have been allowed to come in and look around. It turned out to be a pretty cool room after all.

We love and appreciate these marines and corpsmen for their sacrifice they gave for us, and they will always be in our thoughts and prayers. I am so glad that everyone who reads this book will get to meet the men of Kilo Company 3/3/3 through their stories and realize what they gave of themselves to help keep America free. Please keep them in your prayers. If you meet a veteran or current service member, thank them for serving our country.

—Laura Clark

Afterword

Adopt a Freedom Fighter

The effectual fervent prayer of a righteous man availed much. (James5:16, KJV)

If any man see his brother sin a sin which is not unto death, he shall ask, and He shall give him life for them that sin not unto death. (1John 5:16, KJV)

Operation Adopt a Freedom Fighter Standing in the Gap for Our Troops

After the terrorist attack in America on September 11, 2001, I found myself wanting to do something to stand in support of our country. Knowing that I was limited by my PTSD problems and my age, the list of possibilities were small, but I kept on looking anyway. A friend told me there was an opening at our local police department to become a chaplain for the officers, and I seized the opportunity. It worked out good for a while until the added stress of working with law enforcement began to cause me adrenaline problems. I was forced to give it up after only a few months and let the younger generation take over my position. I continued praying for God's leading as to what he would have me to do, and soon, the answer came.

It was "use what you have."

My experiences in Vietnam were what I really have, and God wanted me to use them for a positive message rather than a negative one. I truly believe my life was preserved in Vietnam through

ADVhm

the prayers of my father to a loving God, and I was ultimately the undeserving benefactor. That concept of intercessory prayer warrior could possibly be used for others.

Beginning the Project

I soon began formulating the basis for the idea of Operation Adopt a Freedom Fighter. Being that I couldn't go with the marines, sailors, and soldiers to fight in Iraq and Afghanistan, I could be with and support them in concentrated prayer. It had worked with my dad, and there was no reason for it not working now. I put together a plan of action for going to churches, schools, VFWs, or anywhere else they would allow me to speak to them. I would explain my idea to as many as would listen, and maybe others would join me. It was a good concept and worth a try.

The word *adopt* simply means to choose or take as one's own. The idea would be for the volunteer to choose a name from a list of warriors and pray for them as one of their own children. They would never have contact or meet the soldier in person, but they would cover them in prayer every day. My dad didn't know what was going on in my life, but he just prayed and trusted God to take care of me. That's what we'd be doing too.

1. I began to make a list of military personnel who were going overseas. Most of the names came from a client list my wife had in her cake-topper business. I asked each one who called to place a cake-topper order for their permission to add their name to the prayer list. Ninety-nine percent of those who I talked with gladly gave their permission and thought it was a great idea to cover them and their families in prayer in such a volatile time. We were honored to do so.

2. I began to advertise my plan to churches in my area through fliers and the use of Christian radio. It worked really well because it wasn't long before invitations began coming in. I began going all over North Carolina to speak to congregations. It was a little nerve-racking for me at the beginning to stand in front of large crowds, but the lives of so many American fighting men and women were on the line, and I knew it was important, so I pushed on.

My Presentation

I began by talking about deadly combat and how fearful it can become when you're about to die on a battlefield thousands of miles from home. I had to show them the reality of what battle really feels like in order to show them the miracles that God had performed in my life. There were many for me to choose from, but I tried to keep it down to two different situations where I thought I was going to die. It was amazing and sometimes humorous to see how God worked out his will over the battle scene to keep me safe. The audience would laugh and cry at times as they watched the miracles unfold before them. Without a doubt, God was ultimately the one who got the glory for the victorious outcome. I tried to make sure the audience knew I didn't have all the answers, and no one knows why some die in battle and some live. Only God knows the answers to some things, and we're better off if we allow his will to be done. I would tell them the true story of Robert and Josh and how Josh was reaching out to God as he succumbed to a gunshot wound to his head.

Regardless of what his past had been and what others knew about him, I believe he found the Lord on the spot where he died. Josh reached out by faith, and God accepted him as his own. Someone was praying for Josh, and their prayers were answered even though they never knew the outcome. God was faithful to answer, and Josh, like me, was the undeserving benefactor. Praise the Lord! I know that Adopt a Freedom Fighter has been used to support many Americans fighting to keep our country free. It is just another way that we can do something to help our men and women come back home to us victorious. I encourage anyone who wants to use this program to create support for those who are protecting us at home to do so. We all need to continue finding a way of supporting our troops at home and abroad. We must have God's help in winning the war on terrorism, and we must not procrastinate any longer. Pray, be creative, and get busy.

Still in the Fight

Ray is finally living a good and productive life alongside of his wife, Laura. He has learned in recent years to slow down to enjoy the privilege of growing old and take one day at a time. It has taken years of struggling and a lot of trial and errors before he could find effective ways to cope with his adrenaline addiction and disorder he developed in Vietnam. The coping skills that are included in this book are not for amusement or to merely take up space—they are for survival. Through them, he has learned to adapt, improvise, and overcome the debilitating effects of post-traumatic stress disorder. Along with the Veterans Administration, his success and happiness primarily involves his relationship with his two closest friends, Jesus Christ and Laura. He spends much of his time with both of them as they are the love of his life. Ray stays busy and invests much of his time sharing his love for Christ and his testimony of how God intervened in sparing his life in combat to congregations everywhere. The primary focus of the inspirational program is called Adopt a Freedom Fighter, where Ray admonishes audiences to support our troops in concentrated, intercessory prayer. The prayer initiative for standing in the gap for our service members has appeared on television and talk on radio programs in North Carolina. It is a unique way we can all participate in war against terrorism. Once a marine, always a marine. Ray has never stopped fighting for just causes, and he plans to continue reaching out to America's walking wounded through his own narrative, *The Never-Ending War*. Though his dream of writing his memoir is finished, it will probably not be the last thing he does as he is always looking for another way to serve his country.

Appendix

Marine Infantry Command Structure

- Fire team—four individual marines assigned to a designated team.

- Squad—three four-man fire teams assigned to a squad.

- Platoon—three squads assigned to a specific rifle platoon.

- Company—three infantry platoons make up a rifle company.

- Battalion—three or four rifle companies along with a weapons, headquarters, and

- service company make up a battalion.

- Regiment—three or more infantry battalions comprise a regiment.

- Division—three infantry regiments are assigned to a division.

- Marine Corps—three or more divisions and air wing make up the Marine Corps.

- It is the smallest branch of America's military forces but known for its legendary fighting esprit de corps and semper fidelis (Never give up).

★★★

It doesn't matter how big the dog is in the fight. It only matters how big the fight is in the dog. Oorah!

Murphy's Law of Combat

1. If the enemy is in range, so are you.

2. Never intentionally draw fire. It makes everyone around you mad.

3. Try to look unimportant, the enemy may be low on ammunition.

4. Never salute or get saluted when in the bush. It may be the last thing you do.

5. The easy way is usually the most dangerous way.

6. The enemy invariably attacks on two occasions:

   a. When you're ready for them.

   b. When you're not ready for them.

7. Anything you do can get you shot—including nothing.

8. Never share a fighting hole with someone who is not afraid to die.

9. Never walk when you can stand. Never stand when you can sit. Never sit when you can lie down. Never just lie down when you can get a power nap. And never pass up a resupply of clean water.

10. Stay alert and always expect the unexpected.

11. Never share a fighting hole with an atheist.

12. Try to make as few mistakes as possible. You will have to live with yourself for the rest of your life.

The Never-Ending War by Raymond Clark is the memoirs of Raymond Clark. It is written by Laura Clark. All rights reserved.

Personal contributions, personal narratives, post-traumatic stress studies, Veterans Administration Information Center, Marine Corps Historical Center, Marine Corps Basic Training Manual, Murphy's Law of Combat, Marine Corps Records Center in Quantico, Virginia, Audie Murphy Research Foundation, Vietnamese Conflict 1961–1975. psychological aspects.

Scripture quotations are taken from the Holy Bible (KJV). Many fictitious names have been used throughout the book to protect the confidentiality of those we could not reach for consent.

Glossary

- Chicom—short for Chinese Communist grenade.

- Claymore mine—a directional, electrically detonated antipersonnel mine used on approaching enemy troops.

- Fighting hole—the same as fox hole. Only foxes hide in fox holes, and marines fight in fighting holes. It's a marine thing.

- Gook—though seldom spoken in modern times due to it being an inflammatory slang directed toward Asian people, it was a term that marines in contact used as a quick reference to enemy troops. Using longer references in dire situations such as "enemy combatant or NVA soldier" would have gotten us killed. We had no time to use political correctness in the jungles of Vietnam.

- M60—an ammunition belt fed medium machine gun used by American forces in Vietnam.

- Medevac—a term used for medical evacuation of wounded troops.

- RPG—a shoulder-held, rocket-propelled grenade used by Communist forces.